Starting Early with
Study Skills

STARTING EARLY WITH STUDY SKILLS

A Week-by-Week Guide for Elementary Students

Judith L. Irvin
Florida State University

Elaine O. Rose
Rose Speech and Academic Center
Tallahassee, Florida

Allyn and Bacon
Boston   London   Toronto   Sydney   Tokyo   Singapore

Library of Congress Cataloging-in-Publication Data

Irvin, Judith L.
   Starting early with study skills : a week-by-week guide for elementary students / Judith L. Irvin, Elaine O. Rose.
      p.   cm.
   Includes bibliographical references and index.
   ISBN 0-205-13943-4
   1. Study skills--Handbooks, manuals, etc.   2. Education, Elementary--Handbooks, manuals, etc.   I. Rose, Elaine O.
II. Title.
LB1610.I78   1994
371.3' 028'12--dc20   94-346
                                                              CIP

Printed in the United States of America

10   9   8   7   6   5   4   3   2   98   97   96

Contents

Goals of Suggested Classroom Activities   ix

List of Student Activities   xi

Preface   xv

About the Authors   xvii

Chapter 1   Defining the Study Skills   1

    The Process of Studying   3
    Getting Students Organized   3
    Extracting Information   4
    Organizing Information   5
    Demonstrating an Understanding and Application of Knowledge   5

    How to Use This Book   6
    Summary   9

Chapter 2   Learning and Remembering   10

    Strategic Learning   11
    Metacognition   12
    Metacognition and Studying   12
    Schema Theory   13
    The Role of the Teacher   14
    Summary   15

    SUGGESTED CLASSROOM ACTIVITIES   16

GETTING STUDENTS ORGANIZED

Chapter 3   Fostering Student Independence   23

    Organizing Student Desks and Notebooks   25

Following a Daily Schedule   25

Unit Approach   26

Organization at Home   28

Understanding Learning Preferences   29

Summary   30

SUGGESTED CLASSROOM ACTIVITIES   31

EXTRACTING INFORMATION

Chapter 4   Preparing Students to Read   51

Kinds of Text   52

Identifying and Remembering Main Ideas   54

Key Words   55

Flexible Reading   56

Summary   57

SUGGESTED CLASSROOM ACTIVITIES   58

Chapter 5   Promoting Active Reading   72

Strategies to Promote Active Reading   74

Self-Questioning   74
INSERT   75
Underlining/Highlighting   76
SQ3R   76
Summary   77

SUGGESTED CLASSROOM ACTIVITIES   78

Chapter 6   Promoting Active Listening   96

Research in Listening Comprehension   97

Listening and Reading Comprehension   98

Teaching Listening Comprehension   98

Strategies to Promote Active Listening   99

Summary   100

SUGGESTED CLASSROOM ACTIVITIES   101

ORGANIZING INFORMATION

Chapter 7   Taking Useful Notes   125

Research on Note-Taking   126

Teaching Note-Taking   127

Using Charts to Organize Information   **128**
Summary   **128**

SUGGESTED CLASSROOM ACTIVITIES   **130**

Chapter 8   Making and Using Maps   147
Theoretical Basis of Mapping   148
Teaching Mapping   149
Summary   149

SUGGESTED CLASSROOM ACTIVITIES   **150**

DEMONSTRATING KNOWLEDGE

Chapter 9   Answering Essay Questions and
Writing Summaries and Reports   173
Writing to Learn   174
Answering Essay Questions   175
Writing Good Summaries   175
Research on Summarizing   176
Teaching Summary Writing   176
Writing Good Reports   177
Teaching Report Writing   178
Summary   179

SUGGESTED CLASSROOM ACTIVITIES   **180**

Chapter 10   Taking Tests   204
Teaching Test-Taking Skills   205
Improving Memory   206
Taking Vocabulary Tests   207
Summary   208

SUGGESTED CLASSROOM ACTIVITIES   **209**

References   242

Index   247

Goals of Suggested Classroom Activities

WEEK 1
16

GOALS
1. Increase awareness of study skills through self-monitoring.
2. Increase motivation to learn and to remember.
3. Improve organizational ability through a Study Skills Notebook.

WEEK 2
31

GOALS
1. Organize student desks.
2. Begin to use a work folder.
3. Begin to use an assignment sheet.
4. Increase awareness of appropriate home study skills.
5. Use scheduling/goal-setting techniques.
6. Increase awareness of learning styles.

WEEK 3
58

GOALS
1. Understand text structure (narrative and expository).
2. Understand book parts.
3. Understand paragraph structure.
4. Use flexible reading rates.

WEEKS 4 and 5
78

GOAL
1. Develop active reading through:
   a. Self-questioning
   b. INSERT
   c. Highlighting
   d. SQ3R

WEEK 6
101

GOAL
1. Develop active listening through:
   a. Understanding the difference between listening and hearing
   b. Setting a purpose for listening
   c. Listening games
   d. Listening for details and main ideas
   e. Predicting
   f. TQLR

WEEKS 7 and 8   **130**

GOAL   *1.* *Develop note-taking skills for expository tests through:*
      a. *Divided page*
      b. *Cornell Notetaking Method*
      c. *Charts*
      d. *Index cards*
      e. *Use of Abbreviations*

WEEKS 9 and 10   **150**

GOAL   *1.* *Develop note-taking skills for narrative text through story maps and character analysis.*
    2. *Develop note-taking skills for expository text through chapter maps.*

WEEKS 11 through 14   **180**

GOAL   *1.* *Develop writing skills for summaries, reports, and essays through:*
      a. *Organizing ideas before writing*
      b. *Writing a good introduction, including facts, and writing a good conclusion*
      c. *Using transition words and adjectives*
      d. *Editing*
      e. *Reading the essay question carefully and underlining key words*

WEEKS 15 and 16   **209**

GOAL   *1.* *Develop objective test-taking skills by:*
      a. *Improving memory*
      b. *Understanding the types of test questions*
      c. *Understanding test question format*
      d. *Learning how to take objective tests*

List of Student Activities

1   *How to Be a Better Student*   18
2   *Study Skills Checklist*   19
3   *Self-Monitoring Checklist*   22
4   *Friday System*   34
5   *Places to Study*   36
6   *Long-Term Goals*   37
7   *Goals for This Week*   38
8   *General Assignment Sheet*   39
9   *Assignment Pad by Class*   41
10 *Weekly Calendar*   43
11 *Monthly Calendar*   44
12 *How You Spend Your Time*   46
13 *Homework*   48
14 *Hints for Homework*   49
15 *Ways We Learn*   50
16 *Study Skills Review 1*   61
17 *Two Types of Text*   62
18 *Book Scavenger Hunt*   63
19 *Paragraph Structure*   64
20 *Paragraph Structure in Expository Text*   65
21 *Paragraph Structure—Writing Your Own*   67
22 *Paragraph Purpose*   68
23 *Reading Rate—An Analogy*   70
24 *Key Words*   71
25 *Study Skills Review 2*   82
26 *Self-Questioning—Narrative Text*   84
27 *Self-Questioning—Expository Text*   86
28 *KWL Chart*   88
29 *Writing Test Questions*   90
30 *INSERT Method*   91
31 *Highlighting*   93
32 *SQ3R Guide*   94
33 *Matching SQ3R with Purpose*   95
34 *Listening and Hearing*   110
35 *Self-Questioning—Listening*   111
36 *Self-Questioning with Expository Text*   112
37 *Fill in the Blanks While Listening*   114

38 *Writing Questions*   *115*
39 *TQLR with Coca-Cola*   *116*
40 *TQLR Review*   *119*
41 *The Steps of TQLR*   *121*
42 *Listening to Answer Questions*   *123*
43 *Study Skills Review 3*   *134*
44 *Unorganized Words*   *136*
45 *Organized Words*   *137*
46 *Divided Page Notes*   *138*
47 *Using Cornell Notetaking System 1*   *139*
48 *Cornell Notetaking*   *140*
49 *Using Abbreviations*   *142*
50 *Using Cornell Notetaking System 2*   *143*
51 *Using Charts 1*   *145*
52 *Using Charts 2*   *146*
53 *Study Skills Review 4*   *157*
54 *Character Map*   *159*
55 *Compare/Contrast Chart*   *161*
56 *Story Map*   *163*
57 *Story Frame*   *165*
58 *Plot Relationships Chart*   *166*
59 *Story Summary*   *167*
60 *Mapping Florida's Beginnings*   *168*
61 *Character Map on Florida's Beginnings*   *169*
62 *Mapping Storms*   *170*
63 *Map of Storms*   *171*
64 *Study Skills Checklist*   *184*
65 *Writing a Good Summary 1*   *185*
66 *Writing a Good Summary 2*   *187*
67 *Outline of Your Life*   *189*
68 *Transition Words*   *191*
69 *Editing Checklist*   *192*
70 *Map of a Famous Person*   *193*
71 *Editing Checklist*   *195*
72 *Essay Terms*   *196*
73 *Practice with Essay Terms*   *197*
74 *How to Write a Good Answer to an Essay Question*   *198*
75 *Review of Essay Writing Steps*   *199*
76 *Answering Good Essay Questions 1*   *200*
77 *Answering Good Essay Questions 2*   *202*
78 *Improving Concentration*   *214*
79 *Increasing Memory*   *216*
80 *Review of Memory Aids*   *218*
81 *Practice with Mnemonics*   *220*
82 *Types of Questions*   *221*
83 *What Type of Question? 1*   *223*
84 *What Type of Question? 2*   *225*

85 *Multiple-Choice Steps   227*
86 *Multiple-Choice Practice   228*
87 *Answering True-False Questions   230*
88 *Completion and Matching   232*
89 *Vocabulary Tests   234*
90 *Spelling Tests   236*
91 *Taking an Objective Test   238*
92 *Review of Test Taking   239*
93 *Study Skills Coat of Arms   241*

Preface

Most educators would agree that learning study skills is important and that such skills are generally taught in one form or another throughout a child's educational experience. We believe, however, that even young students can learn to study effectively. *Starting Early with Study Skills: A Week-by-Week Guide for Elementary Students* is for teachers, curriculum specialists, and administrators who advocate beginning early with systematic instruction in study skills.

This book is consistent with current research and theory in learning and remembering; concepts such as schema and metacognition pervade suggested classroom and student activities. Relevant research is discussed at the beginning of the chapters. Then, week-by-week outlines of suggested classroom activities are presented. Last, reproducible student activities provide a systematic study skills program for elementary students. Teachers may choose to proceed week by week through the program or they may wish to use the chapters to teach important concepts using materials of their own to supplement suggested activities.

We have not made the distinction between "primary" activities and "intermediate" activities. We use high-interest material in all of the activities and assume that teachers will make the necessary adjustments for students of varying abilities.

We hope you find this book useful as you provide study skills instruction for elementary school children.

ACKNOWLEDGMENTS

We would like to thank the following reviewers for their comments and suggestions: Joan Baker, Cleveland State University; Kathy Everts Danielson, University of Nebraska at Omaha; Linda Grippando, Downers Grove School System in Downers Grove, Illinois; Marcia Modlo, Vestal Schools, Vestal, New York; and Fred Schroeder, Assistant Superintendent of Schools in Schaumburg, Illinois.

For us, this project became a family venture. Our thanks to Bruce, Brandon, Alesha, John, Joey, and Keri for their lessons and input on this project. In addition, we would like to thank Laura Franco, who patiently provided assistance on the many revisions of the student activities.

J. L. I.
E. O. R.

About the Authors

Judith L. Irvin teaches at Florida State University in Tallahassee, Florida. She is Chair of the Research Committee of the National Middle School Association and editor of *Research in Middle Level Education*. Among her most notable books are *Reading and the Middle School Student: Strategies to Enhance Literacy* (Allyn and Bacon), *Vocabulary Knowledge: Guidelines for Instruction* (National Education Association), *Transforming Middle Level Education: Perspectives and Possibilities* (Allyn and Bacon), *Leadership in Middle Level Education* (National Association of Secondary School Principals), and *Enhancing Social Studies Through Literacy Strategies* (National Council for the Social Studies). She is also a member of the authorship team for the *HBJ Treasury of Literature* basal series (Harcourt Brace Publishing Company) and has authored numerous articles. Dr. Irvin has consulted nationally and internationally in middle school literacy, curriculum and instructional reform efforts, and leadership issues.

Elaine O. Rose is the owner/director of a large, private academic clinic in Tallahassee, Florida. The clinic serves children from preschool through college, working in the areas of reading, math, writing, and study skills. Ms. Rose has helped train school personnel in the teaching of study skills at the elementary level, and has taught both regular and remedial classes at the first-, fourth-, and fifth-grade levels. In addition, she has extensive training in the diagnosis and remediation of reading difficulties, and the application of good study skills techniques. She has also taught teacher education courses focusing on study skills and reading for Florida State University. Ms. Rose has worked more than 20 years with students who struggle in school. This background has led to the creation of this book and her desire that the techniques taught will help students have a more successful school career.

Chapter
1
Defining the Study Skills

Overview
Study skills involve the ability to extract information and organize it in such a way as to demonstrate understanding and application of that knowledge at a later time.

Study skills: Everyone wants them, students need them, educators extol them, and hardly anyone seems to teach them systematically. To be successful, students must be able to organize themselves and their learning, to extract and organize information, and to demonstrate understanding and application of that knowledge at a later time. Students can use this newly acquired knowledge as prior knowledge for further inquiry. But how do students attain proficiency in study skills?

Study skills are usually considered to be acquired, and typically taught, at the secondary level. A foundation, however, can be laid in the elementary grades, even as early as kindergarten. Most educators would agree that study skills need to be taught systematically and reinforced throughout the elementary grades. But what is meant by the term *study skills?*

Learning for remembering—that is, studying—involves reading and listening for meaning and much more. Learners who have in mind a specific academic goal must be able to select important ideas from a text or oral presentation and organize these ideas to remember them later. In short, students must know *how* to remember information and know *what* information to remember.

The effectiveness of study strategies depends on two factors:

- How actively students process information while engaging in learning activities

- How knowledgeable students are of the task they are to perform

A student may take notes by copying the author's words in a passive way or by actively summarizing ideas while constructing a chapter map. How a student takes notes also depends on what he or she will do with the information. Studying for an objective test requires attention to detail; studying for an essay requires an understanding of the overall concepts. So, effective study requires active involvement and an understanding of what is to be done with the newly acquired information.

The academic tasks for which study skills are required are familiar to students and teachers alike. They include multiple-choice or essay exams, research papers, book reports, and speeches; these goals are sometimes called *criterion tasks*. "When the criterion task is made explicit to the students before they read the text, students will learn more from studying than when the criterion task remains vague" (Anderson & Armbruster, 1984, p. 658). To study effectively and efficiently, students must have enough information about the task at hand to determine what and how to study. Using study strategies effectively and having a realistic expectation of the criterion task lead to another benefit for students—learning.

Students often distinguish between school and *real life*. Study skills, perhaps more than many other things learned in school, have a direct application to *real life*. Listening to a radio news broadcast, watching a NOVA program on whales, or organizing your desk to pay bills all require certain abilities that may fall under the heading of *study skills*.

THE PROCESS OF STUDYING

Studying and learning are essentially the same process, except that studying also includes later performance on a particular task. It is important to teachers that students perform well on tests and assignments. But the *process* of learning is just as important as the *product*. That is, to achieve the desired outcome, attention must be focused on the means. The story of Joey and his mother illustrates how the use of efficient study skills facilitates learning.

> *Joey, a fourth-grader, was having trouble in social studies. After several attempts to pass tests, he finally asked his mother, a reading teacher, for help. He wanted his mother to teach him the information so that he could perform well on the next test. His mother taught Joey to cluster the information into a chapter map and to learn the definitions of key words using the divided page format. After an hour of organizing the information, Joey was disgusted; he felt that he had not even begun to "study" for the test. He left the table and went upstairs with his chapter map and divided page notes. His parting comment was, "I don't have time for all of this; I have to* learn *this stuff."*
>
> *Wondering if he would ever learn to study, Joey's mother later heard him emerge from his room and exclaim, "Mom, when you do all this before studying, you know the stuff so well, you don't have to study!"*

What Joey had discovered was that if information is organized into meaningful units, it is easier to understand the concepts and remember them. Memorizing isolated information becomes unnecessary and inefficient. By organizing and relating information, concepts are understood and remembered. More about organizing information will be discussed later in this book.

Getting Students Organized

> *Brian never has a pencil. When asked to look through his desk to find something to write with, Brian is lost in a sea of old papers, lost assignments, pieces of leftover candy, and overdue library books. Brian's class work is usually late, if it gets completed at all. He seems unaware of when tests are given or how to study for them. Homework is never turned in and Brian's parents are unsupportive. In short, Brian lacks purpose and organization.*

One of the most important aspects of effective study is organization. Elementary teachers can do much to facilitate the organizational ability of their students. Teachers can help and encourage students to maintain an orderly desk, fill out an assignment/homework sheet, draw up and adhere to a schedule, and set achievable goals. These tasks, which are all factors in helping students get and stay organized for maximum learning, are discussed in Chapter 3.

Extracting Information

> *Stephanie was delighted to receive an invitation to Lauren's slumber party. The party was still on her mind as she opened her science book to read the assigned chapter on reptiles. Her mind continued to drift from the ramblings of reptiles to the pleasure of a party. When Stephanie finished "reading," she looked at the questions at the end of the chapter. The first question was, "Are reptiles warm-blooded?" Stephanie did not know what* warm-blooded *meant. She tried the next question. "Are snakes reptiles?" She remembered something about snakes, but was not sure if she had read whether or not they were reptiles. Stephanie looked over the rest of the questions and realized she could answer only a few of them. The next day, she went to her teacher in frustration and exclaimed, "I don't understand this chapter. It is too confusing."*

Stephanie, like many students, has not learned the importance of being an active reader. She went through the motions of reading, but her comprehension was poor because her mind was not focused on the text.

Before a student begins reading or listening, it is important that he or she has an appropriate mind-set. Students must focus their attention on what they are to read and put aside distracting thoughts and ideas. One technique for activating students' interest (and thus attention) involves *previewing* or *surveying* the text, or thinking about the topic the teacher will discuss. This engages students' prior knowledge and helps students to anticipate what they will read. Previewing can also serve to help students learn new words, decide on an appropriate reading rate, and choose the type of notes that may be necessary to maximize remembering.

Extracting information also requires an awareness of text; this awareness helps to develop the proper mind-set for reading. Narrative text has a different structure, involves different tasks, and allows a different rate of reading than does expository text. Thus, students must approach literature selections in a different manner than they would approach a science text. These topics are discussed in Chapter 4.

To facilitate the deep processing of text or spoken language, students must carefully monitor their understanding. Self-questioning, the INSERT method of promoting active reading, and highlighting are three ways of helping students become active readers. These methods are explained in Chapter 5.

Effective listening can maximize success in learning. In addition, activities to facilitate listening comprehension have also been found to improve reading comprehension. It is important that students are able to construct meaning from orally presented information, as well as from a text. Promoting active listening comprehension is discussed in Chapter 6.

Organizing Information

> *Tad, a student with learning disabilities who has weak memory skills, usually does well in science because he finds the experiments and ideas fascinating. When he was asked to read a difficult chapter on violent storms, however, he became frustrated. In desperation, he talked with his father. "I just can't learn all this information. I don't remember which storms occur in which months, how fast each storm travels, and where they form. It is just too much to memorize." After an hour of trying to drill Tad with facts, both father and son gave up in frustration. If Tad or his father had known some simple techniques for organizing information into manageable memory units, the science lesson would have been more interesting and Tad would have understood and remembered much more.*

Once information is read or heard, students must organize the information. One key component to organizing information involves separating main ideas and important details from less important information. The information thus selected is organized into "memory units" in the form of notes, which make the ideas read or heard permanent and ready for retrieval. The act of writing the notes helps students learn the information. Graphic organizers, including semantic maps, are another excellent way of organizing information. These techniques can be introduced in kindergarten and used, with increasing sophistication, through college. Chapters 7 and 8 discuss the advantages of several methods of organizing information such as divided page note-taking system and using charts and maps.

Demonstrating an Understanding and Application of Knowledge

> *Cindy has always been considered a good student and has scored well on standardized tests, especially in reading. In third grade, however, her test scores dropped significantly in reading comprehension. Knowing that the end-of-the-year standardized test was approaching, Cindy's teacher decided to investigate the difficulty. Analysis of the test booklet revealed that Cindy consistently missed main idea and inference questions. When Cindy's teacher asked her about a specific inference question she missed, Cindy responded that the passage never told her the answer to that question, so she just picked one of the facts she remembered from the story. Cindy gave the same rationale for her answer to the main idea question. Cindy did not know how to figure out answers to questions that were not directly stated in the passage. With a few brief lessons on types of test questions and how to "think" of an answer that is not directly stated, Cindy's comprehension scores were brought up and remained high.*

Students are tested from the time they enter preschool until the time they graduate from college. As students get older and more sophisticated, the questions become more diverse and complicated. Students must become "test-wise" in order to deal effectively with a variety of questions and tasks. Good test scores should not be reserved for the students who figure out the system on their own. Students also need direct instruction in how to write a good report, using appropriate main ideas and supporting details. Chapters 9 and 10 focus on methods to help students demonstrate the knowledge they have when they answer essay questions, write summaries or reports, and take tests.

HOW TO USE THIS BOOK

The purpose of this book is to help teachers teach students to study more efficiently. The following Study Skills Checklist represents the components of effective study skill instruction. Teachers of upper elementary students may want to copy this checklist and keep a copy for each student and check off each skill as the student demonstrates mastery. Specific suggestions for student activities are made throughout this book that are consistent with our definition of study skills.

Study Skills Checklist

    I. Becomes an Active Learner
        A. Reads actively
        B. Listens actively
        C. Finds meanings of new words
        D. Asks questions
        E. Tries hard
    II. Gets and Stays Organized
        A. Organizes desk
        B. Maintains notebook
            1. Uses assignment pad
            2. Uses monthly calendar
            3. Uses work folder
        C. Gets outside monitoring, if necessary
            1. Gets assignment pad signed
            2. Uses Friday system
        D. Follows schedule
        E. Organizes home studying
            1. Uses quiet, comfortable place
            2. Has necessary supplies
            3. Sets aside time to study
            4. Takes short breaks

          5. Sets up study schedule to complete projects and book reports

          6. Reviews notes even when there is not a test

     F. Sets goals and schedules

     G. Understands learning preferences

III. Understands Text Structure

     A. Narrative

     B. Expository

IV. Uses Flexible Reading Rates

V. Understands Book Parts

VI. Understands Paragraphs

     A. Structure

          1. Main idea, then details

          2. Detail, then main idea

          3. Details, main idea, details

          4. No main idea or implied idea

          5. Main idea, details, main idea

     B. Purpose

          1. Get reader's interest

          2. Give facts

          3. Give main ideas

VII. Actively Reads

     A. Self-Questioning

     B. Highlighting

     C. SQ3R

          1. Survey

          2. Question

          3. Read

          4. Recite

          5. Review

VIII. Actively Listens

     A. Sits in front when possible

     B. Concentrates

     C. Asks questions

IX. Uses Notetaking

     A. Expository

          1. Divided page

          2. Cornell Method

          3. Mapping

          4. Charts

          5. Index cards

          6. Abbreviates

      B. Narrative

          1. Story maps

          2. Character analysis

  X. Uses Memory/Concentration Techniques

      A. Recites

      B. Writes

      C. Mnemonics

  XI. Uses Good Writing Skills for Reports and Essays

      A. Reads the question accurately

      B. Organizes information before writing

      C. Writes using a good introduction, details, and a good conclusion

      D. Uses transition words and adjectives

      E. Edits

  XII. Uses Good Test-Taking Skills for Objective Tests

      A. Types of questions

          1. Multiple choice

          2. Matching

          3. True/false

          4. Completion

      B. Reduces test anxiety

  XIII. Follows Written Directions Accurately

      A. Underlines key words

      B. Numbers steps

This book addresses four major topics:

- Getting students organized

- Extracting meaningful information

- Organizing information

- Demonstrating understanding and application of that knowledge at a later time

Each chapter has three parts:

- A discussion of the issues related to each topic
- Suggested classroom activities
- Reproducible pages for student activities

Some of the student activity pages are more difficult than others and may be more suitable for intermediate students than primary students. We have made a deliberate attempt not to have some pages seem "too primary" or "too intermediate" so that teachers will be able to use the full range of suggested activities.

Some teachers may decide to "lift" activities to incorporate in their existing study skills program. Other teachers may wish to follow all of the suggested activities week by week. For those teachers who choose to follow all of the suggested activities, we highly suggest maintaining a Study Skills Notebook for all student work. We hope that you will find this book helpful as you help students learn and remember more effectively.

SUMMARY

From the intermediate grades through college, students are often expected to spend a great deal of time reading content area textbooks, listening and taking notes, and taking tests. Often, the foundation is not laid in the elementary grades for students to be successful with these independent learning tasks. Study strategies are necessary to help students take charge of their own learning. Therefore, the systematic teaching of study skills during the elementary grades is of paramount importance.

Chapter
2
Learning and Remembering

Overview

Strategic learning involves (1) cognitive skills (knowledge of study skills) and metacognition (awareness and conscious control of when and how to use study skills); (2) schema theory (making sense of new information by relating it to information that is already known); (3) integrating instruction (applying what is learned in one area to another area that aids learning); and (4) techniques to aid learning, such as Think-Pair-Share.

Lisa, a fifth-grade student, was having difficulty in school with all subjects that involved reading. Her test scores showed a significant comprehension weakness. Lisa could read isolated words and understand the meanings of these words on or above grade level, but she had difficulty comprehending natural text at even the third-grade level. Lisa's teacher began a program to improve her comprehension, which included increasing Lisa's self-monitoring ability, developing a flexible reading rate, and identifying important ideas. Lisa's comprehension improved. After about three weeks, Lisa seemed to understand; she looked up with a smile and said, "So, you want me to remember what I read."

Effective and efficient learning leads to increased remembering, especially if students understand ahead of time the purpose of their task. If students are taught to learn in an organized manner, their ability to remember that information and their performance on later tasks will be more successful.

Learning in which students also "remember" is strategic or deliberate. *Strategic learning* involves using *metacognition* to evaluate and monitor learning and using *schema or prior knowledge* to connect new to known information. These constructs have been developed over the last decade to help educators understand the learning process and to help students become independent, lifelong learners. In the following few pages, we will discuss these important constructs as they relate to the teaching of study skills and the role of the teacher in developing these abilities in students.

STRATEGIC LEARNING

A *strategy* is a conscious effort on the part of the learner to attend to comprehension while reading, listening, or participating in any learning event. It may be helpful to distinguish between the term *strategies* and the more traditional term *skills*.

- *Strategies* emphasize intentional and deliberate plans; *skills* are more automatic.

- *Strategies* emphasize reasoning and cognitive sophistication; *skills* are associated with lower levels of thinking and learning.

- *Strategies* are flexible and adaptable; *skills* connote consistency in application across tasks.

- *Strategies* imply an awareness or reflection on what they are doing while learning; *skills* imply an automatic response to learning (Dole, Duffy, Roehler, & Pearson, 1991, p. 242).

An emerging skill can become a strategy when it is used intentionally (Paris, Wasik, & Turner, 1991). Strategic learners know whether or not they understand what they read or what they hear and are willing to use any of a number of available strategies to help them understand better. Over a period of years (and, it is hoped, beginning with early learning experiences), efficient learners may develop many strategies to help them construct meaning.

METACOGNITION

Learning is often referred to as a cognitive event, but it is important to note that it is also a metacognitive event. *Cognition* refers to using the knowledge possessed; *metacognition* refers to a person's awareness and understanding of that knowledge. "Cognition refers to having the skills; metacognition refers to awareness of and conscious control over those skills" (Stewart & Tei, 1983, p. 36).

When Lisa improved her comprehension, she showed use of cognitive skill. When she became aware that while reading she was to remember what she was reading, she showed evidence of her metacognitive ability. She now had strategies for comprehending and she was aware of these strategies, including when and how to use them.

Lisa had no metacognitive awareness. That is, she did not understand that she was not understanding. Students may thumb through a difficult text while thinking about a school party; *knowing* they are not paying attention to the text is a metacognitive event. Strategic readers would do something— refocus and pay attention, close the book until later, or begin to take notes to organize their thoughts. Good readers who have developed metacognitive awareness do *something*; less proficient readers plow merrily (or not so merrily) along without stopping to assess, question, or correct the condition.

Proficient readers monitor their own comprehension and are able to apply strategies to help them understand, such as rereading, reading ahead, or searching one's prior knowledge to make sense of text. That is, they know when what they are reading is making sense, and they know what to do when it is not making sense. Good listeners also know when speech does not make sense to them; they ask questions, take notes, and/or increase their concentration as they listen. Metacognition develops as a student matures, usually during adolescence, but it can be taught and strengthened by explicit instruction and practice, even at very early ages (Palincsar & Brown, 1983).

METACOGNITION AND STUDYING

When Brandon enters class and sees that the topic for study is volcanoes, metacognition is involved when he assesses what he knows and does not know about the topic. While watching a movie about volcanoes, he makes a mental note of the new information he has learned and makes it "fit" with his prior knowledge or schema for volcanoes. When the teacher explains the terms molten

ash *and* lava, *Brandon notices that he does not completely understand these terms and may be somewhat disturbed because the
information "doesn't fit."*

Studying is an intentional act. Students need to set goals for studying
and put strategies to use when the purpose for studying is to do something
with what was learned, such as study for a test, write a paper, or explain it
to another student (Vacca & Vacca, 1989). While reading a section in the
book on volcanoes, Brandon has two tasks: reading for meaning (monitoring) and reading to remember (selecting appropriate strategies for the task)
(Tonjes, 1991). Before, during, or after reading, Brandon may decide that a
semantic map is the best way to remember and retrieve the information he
has read.

Students who are independent learners know how, why, and when to
use study strategies for specific tasks or assignments. First, they analyze the
task, which includes setting a reading rate and noticing text structure.
Second, they reflect on what they know or do not know about the topic.
Third, they devise a plan for successfully completing the reading and for
evaluating and checking their progress in accomplishing this task (Brown,
1978).

Proficient learners develop these strategies for learning and remembering either on their own or through direct instruction. These deliberate study
strategies, of course, do not occur spontaneously for young and less
proficient readers. Teachers can help young children develop a metacognitive awareness of their learning and an ability to use what they already
know to learn and remember new information.

SCHEMA THEORY

Learning occurs when a student relates new information to what is already
known. It is nearly impossible to learn new information that has no
connection to what is already known. *Schemata* comprise all of the information and all of the experience that the reader has stored in his or her
memory. A particular schema, then, represents all of the associations that
come to mind when a person reads about a certain subject.

For example, you have a schema for the object we label "television."
You have a mental picture of what does or does not characterize a
television. You also bring to that basic picture many other associations. If
you like watching many hours of television, your schema is filled with
positive feelings of limitless entertainment. If you are among the group of
people who feel that the television is an invasion on their free time, you
may have feelings of anxiety or frustration as you think about a television.
One's schema determines the sum total of all of one's thoughts about and
reactions toward a certain subject. A learner cannot separate his or her
schema from what is read; thus, schema influences the interpretation of
what is learned.

Knowledge is organized semantically—like a thesaurus rather than a dictionary (Pearson, 1985). Every student has experienced the frustration of not understanding something because the information presented was outside the realm of anything he or she had learned before. Reading a computer manual may be an example of this frustration. Although the individual words are readily understood, the content area—such as how to set up computer hardware—is disconnected to the reader's schema. The reader is left frustrated and unable to understand.

Our job, as educators, is to help students with this process—to help them learn content and develop their ability to process information at the same time. It is a challenging task for educators to help students understand that the learning processes—reading, writing, speaking, listening, and thinking—can be related to each other, just as bits of knowledge can be related. This type of instruction involves the teacher helping students process information in meaningful ways to help them become independent learners.

One way to make instruction more meaningful to students is to integrate reading instruction with instruction in other language areas. It may seem obvious that all four language systems—reading, writing, speaking, and listening—share the same cognitive and experiential base. Teachers can take advantage of these relationships during instruction. It seems only sensible, then, to teach the language systems together and use as many of the language systems as possible to teach content.

For example, when students are learning about the four food groups, they could first list foods they think are good (writing), classify these foods in groups (thinking), share their groups with others (listening and speaking), read about the four food groups (reading), design menus (writing), write reports on the nutrients in the different food groups (writing), and discuss their reports with other students (speaking and listening). Integrating reading, writing, and content instruction facilitates growth in each area.

THE ROLE OF THE TEACHER

Good learners do not spend a lot of time analyzing their learning behaviors; they just do it naturally. But what can teachers do to facilitate effective reading and writing behavior in their students? The first step is to be concerned about "improving children's comprehension ability rather than just their comprehension" (Johnston, 1985, p. 643). In general, teachers should be more concerned about developing students' ability to learn rather than increase their bank of facts. The goal of instruction should be to produce strategic learners who are as knowledgeable about the process of learning as the material to be learned.

For example, Mason and Au (1990) suggested that teachers discuss with students the role of active thinking in learning and that they help students start lists with headings "Know" and "Don't Know" about a topic of study. Teachers can pause every few sentences so that students can add notes to the lists and then encourage students to adopt this strategy on their own. It is also helpful to students to have the opportunity to share in the cognitive process of teachers and other students.

Think-Pair-Share is a simple, yet elegant, cooperative strategy that facilitates active involvement by all students and provides the opportunity for students to share how they solved problems with each other (McTighe & Lyman, 1988). A question is posed. Students *think* and jot down an answer, then students *pair*. That is, they talk about their answer with a partner. Part of this sharing can be discussing how they arrived at their answer. Then, as a class, they *share* answers. This strategy allows every student an opportunity to answer, at least to a partner. Think-Pair-Share also allows students time to think, respond, and try to make connections with the world they understand.

Opportunities in daily classroom interaction can promote metacognition in students. When teachers take the time to ask students to share how they "figured something out" (a piece of text, a math problem, an answer to a science quiz, etc.), all students benefit from such interaction.

SUMMARY

Students need to learn various study strategies and know what study skill to use and when to use it. Teachers can facilitate learning by helping students relate new information to known information and integrate instruction whenever possible. Activities, such as Think-Pair-Share, have been found to improve the cognitive and metacognitive abilities of students. The activities designed for students in this chapter help students develop metacognitive awareness, monitor their learning, and make connections with what they already know.

SUGGESTED CLASSROOM ACTIVITIES

═══ GOALS ═══

1. *Increase awareness of study skills through self-monitoring.*
2. *Increase motivation to learn and to remember.*
3. *Improve organizational ability through a Study Skills Notebook.*

Week 1

1. Introduce the topic of study skills to your students. Explain that study skills are anything they do that helps them learn and remember. Discuss reading, listening, being organized, doing homework and class work, and studying for tests.

2. Teach the Think-Pair-Share study skill strategy to your students. Ask your students to write things they do that help them learn (such as mapping a science chapter or studying spelling words). After a few minutes, let them share these ideas with another student and then share as a class. Make a list of the study skills they mentioned.

3. Pass out *How to Be a Better Student* (Student Activity 1) and discuss the handout with students, reviewing the five main points (active reading, active listening, meaning of new words, asking questions, and trying hard). Have students use the checklist for the entire day. Remind students during the day to use the checklist and to share the results at the end of the day in small groups, then as a class.

4. Give each student a folder notebook in which they can place paper. Make this a Study Skills Notebook. The first five pages should be as follows:

   Title Page

   Author Page

   Table of Contents

   Study Skills Checklist (Student Activity 2)

   How to Be a Better Student (Student Activity 1)

   Review the entire *Study Skills Checklist* but not in great detail—just enough so students understand the purpose of this unit of study.

5. Let students illustrate the front of their Study Skills Notebook with examples of students using good study habits.

6. Have students use a new copy of *How to Be a Better Student* on several different days to help them become aware of self-monitoring techniques.

7. When students are comfortable monitoring their study skills with the *How to Be a Better Student* checklist, give students the *Self-Monitoring Checklist* (Student Activity 3). This list is a little more advanced, as it divides the school day according to classes. Decide what three class times they will monitor for the day and write the name of the class on the blank under the heading "Class." Use this schedule periodically to encourage self-monitoring. These checklists should be added to the Study Skills Notebook and added to the Table of Contents.

8. In small groups, have students create a list of reasons why homework might not be turned in on time (such as "My dog ate it"). Discuss the validity of each excuse to develop the students' increased awareness of responsibility. Have each student list 10 excuses they will never use again and add this to their Study Skills Notebook.

9. At the end of the first week, have students try to write from memory the five study skill items that they worked on that week (active reading, active listening, learning meanings of new words, asking questions, and trying hard.) After five minutes, let students refer to the original handout. Have students write a summary of the goals they achieved that week. Students should add this summary to their Study Skills Notebook.

Name _____ Date _____

STUDENT ACTIVITY 1

HOW TO BE A BETTER STUDENT

Use this sheet during the day (or week) to record your study skills.

1. Be an *active* reader. Place a check in the box each time you read a passage with real understanding.

2. Be an *active* listener. Each time you listen carefully, place a check in the box.

3. Look for and find the meanings of new words. List new words here. (Use an extra piece of paper if you run out of space.)

_____

_____

_____

4. Ask questions when you do not understand. Place a check in the box each time you ask a question.

5. Try extra hard to do well. Place a check in the box each time you really try hard on an assignment.

Name _____ Date _____

STUDENT ACTIVITY 2

STUDY SKILLS CHECKLIST

I. *Becomes an Active Learner*
   A. Reads actively
   B. Listens actively
   C. Finds meanings of new words
   D. Asks questions
   E. Tries hard
II. *Gets and Stays Organized*
   A. Organizes desk
   B. Maintains notebook
      1. Uses assignment pad
      2. Uses monthly calendar
      3. Uses work folder
   C. Gets outside monitoring, if necessary
      1. Gets assignment pad signed
      2. Uses Friday system
   D. Follows schedule
   E. Organizes home studying
      1. Uses quiet, comfortable place
      2. Has necessary supplies
      3. Sets aside time to study
      4. Takes short breaks
      5. Sets up study schedule to complete projects and book reports
      6. Reviews notes even when there is not a test

(continued)

F. Sets goals and schedules

G. Understands learning preferences

III. *Understands Text Structure*

A. Narrative

B. Expository

IV. *Uses Flexible Reading Rates*

V. *Understands Book Parts*

VI. *Understands Paragraphs*

A. Structure

1. Main idea, then details

2. Detail, then main idea

3. Details, main idea, details

4. No main idea or implied idea

5. Main idea, details, main idea

B. Purpose

1. Get reader's interest

2. Give facts

3. Give main ideas

VII. *Actively Reads*

A. Self-Questioning

B. Highlighting

C. SQ3R

1. Survey

2. Question

3. Read

4. Recite

5. Review

VIII. *Actively Listens*

A. Sits in front when possible

B. Concentrates

C. Asks questions

 IX. *Uses Notetaking*

  A. Expository

   1. Divided page

   2. Cornell Method

   3. Mapping

   4. Charts

   5. Index cards

   6. Abbreviates

  B. Narrative

   1. Story maps

   2. Character analysis

 X. *Uses Memory/Concentration Techniques*

  A. Recites

  B. Writes

  C. Mnemonics

 XI. *Uses Good Writing Skills for Reports and Essays*

  A. Reads the question accurately

  B. Organizes information before writing

  C. Writes using a good introduction, details, and a good conclusion

  D. Uses transition words and adjectives

  E. Edits

 XII. *Uses Good Test-Taking Skills for Objective Tests*

  A. Types of questions

   1. Multiple choice

   2. Matching

   3. True/false

   4. Completion

  B. Reduces test anxiety

 XIII. *Follows Written Directions Accurately*

  A. Underlines key words

  B. Numbers steps

Name _____ Date _____

STUDENT ACTIVITY 3

SELF-MONITORING CHECKLIST

Pick three class times to monitor your own study skills. Write the name of the class under the heading "Class." Now place a check by each study skill that you followed in that class (i.e., listened actively). Think of a way you could have done better in the class and write it down.

Class	___ I listened actively. ___ I read actively. ___ I asked questions. ___ I tried extra hard. ___ I learned at least one new word.	I could have done better by _____ _____ _____
Class	___ I listened actively. ___ I read actively. ___ I asked questions. ___ I tried extra hard. ___ I learned at least one new word.	I could have done better by _____ _____ _____
Class	___ I listened actively. ___ I read actively. ___ I asked questions. ___ I tried extra hard. ___ I learned at least one new word.	I could have done better by _____ _____ _____

Chapter
3
Fostering Student Independence

Overview

Organization is a key to students becoming more independent. Work folders, assignment sheets, and unit booklets are ways of helping students to become more organized. Scheduling, especially homework assignments, helps students use their time more efficiently, and understanding learning preferences helps students to study more effectively.

Jessica, a bright and capable second-grade student, had poor grades, but she could easily do second-grade work. She "forgot" assignments, lost papers, neglected to study for spelling tests because she did not remember to take the book home, and rarely made it to the correct learning center in time. Jessica desperately needed organizational skills and scheduling help.

Her teacher began by helping Jessica clean her desk and organize it in a pyramid style—large books on the bottom with smaller books on top. Jessica was given a work folder. The folder also contained a listing of assignments. On one side of this assignment folder, she kept unfinished work and on the other side went finished work. In the middle, Jessica kept an assignment sheet for her teacher to write his class assignments along with homework assignments and books she needed to carry home.

As Jessica completed her class assignments, she filed them in the "finished" pocket and crossed that assignment off her assignment list. At the end of the day, Jessica checked her assignment list for any work or books to go home that day. At home, Jessica's mother initialed the assignment sheets, indicating that she knew what Jessica was to do. Teacher and parent comments were also passed back and forth this way. Jessica's folder looked like this:

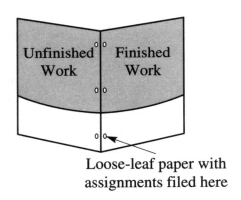

Loose-leaf paper with
assignments filed here

Each day that Jessica had her parents initial the assignment sheet, she received a check on an index card stapled to her folder. Each paper that was completed on time also resulted in a check, as did good spelling grades and a clean desk. At the end of the week, Jessica was able to trade in her checks for library time, free time, time spent in kindergarten as a teacher's reading assistant, or some other reward jointly agreed upon by Jessica, her teacher, and her parents.

The first step in becoming an independent learner is organization. Some students are more organized than others, but organization can be taught to all students. In this chapter, we discuss (1) work folders, assignment sheets, and unit booklets as ways of helping students get organized; and (2) how to help students use time more efficiently and understand their learning preferences.

ORGANIZING STUDENT DESKS AND NOTEBOOKS

Teachers have found the pyramid technique helpful in teaching students to organize themselves and their materials. Basically, all hardback books are placed on one side of the desk, arranged with the largest books on the bottom, so that the student can "see" parts of all books. On the other side of the desk is an assignment folder and a box for supplies. With this system, students can easily find their books. A student desk might look like this:

Desk

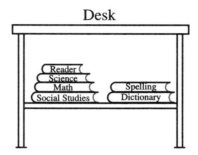

To help students maintain a neat desk in a pyramid style, teachers should have desk checks once a week at a different time each week. Students should not know when the desk checks will occur.

Supplying students with a structured pattern of organizing their desks is an important aid in helping them become efficient learners. Students who have trouble completing their assignments need extra monitoring and help to organize their work in a work folder. They also need to use an assignment sheet. An assignment sheet can be a sheet of notebook paper that lists work to complete or a more formal sheet may be used. Consistent monitoring can help students develop lifelong habits of organization.

FOLLOWING A DAILY SCHEDULE

Activities such as keeping a class calendar, posting a daily schedule on a board, and spending the first few minutes of each day discussing what will happen during the day (using the schedule) and reviewing what actually happened at the end of the day (again using the schedule) helps students become more aware of following a schedule. Students can also be encouraged to keep simple journals or learning logs describing the day's activities. Teachers have found that language experience charts made at the end of the day are helpful in reviewing the day's activities. Students can be given a special schedule of activities of the day listed on an index card taped to the desk. They may use a paper clip that can slide up and down the schedule during the day. A student schedule may look like this:

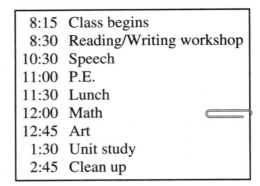

8:15	Class begins
8:30	Reading/Writing workshop
10:30	Speech
11:00	P.E.
11:30	Lunch
12:00	Math
12:45	Art
1:30	Unit study
2:45	Clean up

Assigning nightly homework sheets can help students keep track of materials and assignments. Some teachers give each student a large brown envelope to use as their special homework folder. Parents learn to expect that their children will bring home the "homework folder" daily.

Organizational strategies can be modified for individual students and situations, throughout elementary school and into middle school. The organizing strategies are the following:

1. Help students learn to keep a clean desk (pyramid style) and follow up with random desk checks.

2. Provide students with a work folder with pockets.

3. Show students how to use an assignment pad or sheet, writing assignments in list form and crossing them off when completed.

4. Encourage careful monitoring by parents of those students who need it.

5. Implement a consistent reward program.

6. Provide homework envelopes for students to carry homework back and forth to school.

7. Develop student awareness of schedules.

UNIT APPROACH

Instruction can be more effective if it follows a unit approach, which follows three stages: (1) preinstructional activities, (2) instructional activities, and (3) postinstructional activities. During the *preinstructional phase*, the teacher presents activities designed to motivate the students' interest and activate prior knowledge. This stage is designed to prepare the students for success-ful learning. The *instructional phase* may include reading a text, listening to the teacher or a student explain something, or viewing a film. The *postin-

structional phase includes extension activities—such as writing summaries of what was learned, presenting reports, creating projects, and so on—as a demonstration of the knowledge the student gained during instruction. During this phase, the teacher becomes the coach, evaluating the students and providing additional assistance to those students who are having difficulty.

After progressing through the three stages of instruction, each student should be able to add the information learned to his or her knowledge bank and will also have improved his or her reading, writing, speaking, listening, and/or thinking ability. A brief outline of a unit approach designed to facilitate the content knowledge as well as the development of language abilities follows.

Violent Storms

Preinstruction

1. List as many different storms as you can. Under each of the storm headings, write some key words that go with that type of storm. Share your ideas in a small group.

2. Write synonyms for the word *storm*. Place your words on a continuum, from *violent* to *mild*, such as this:

3. Add suffixes to the word *storm* to create other words.

Instruction

1. Read the chapter on storms in your science textbook to find out more about storms.

2. Create a map. Share your map with a classmate and use his or her information to add to your information. A student map may look like the one shown on page 28.

3. Watch a film on the four types of violent storms. Add this new information to your semantic map.

Postinstruction

1. Using the map, write a summary of each type of storm.

2. Choose one type of storm and draw a picture.

3. Write a creative story that involves a storm.

4. Create three test questions about each of the four types of storms.

Teachers can help students develop organizational skills by having students keep *unit booklets*. As the students create drawings, write research

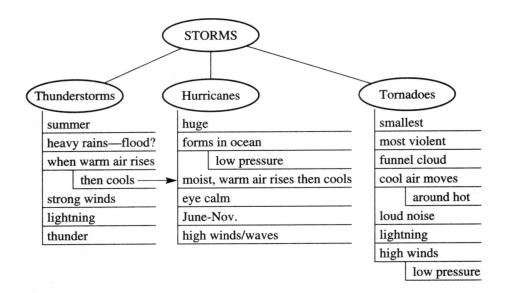

papers, or complete other written activities, these papers are kept in a special booklet that bears the name of the unit of study. For example, if the students are studying clouds, the unit booklet would be named Clouds (which could be shaped like a cumulus cloud when used in the primary grades). Inside the booklet (which could be made of construction paper), the students keep a title page, author page, table of contents, and the activity papers, resources papers, and drawings. As new papers are added to the booklet, a new title is added to the table of contents and the new page is numbered. Unit booklets help students learn to keep material sequentially organized by subject and helps them easily retrieve the information when studying for a test.

ORGANIZATION AT HOME

An important aspect in helping students organize themselves at home is increasing their motivation through goal setting, managing time efficiently, and guidelines to improving home study time. Students are often unaware of why schoolwork is important or, for that matter, what is important to them. Through class discussion and activities, such as setting daily and weekly goals and keeping goal journals, students can become more aware of both short- and long-term goals and what motivates them to work hard to achieve certain goals.

One natural outgrowth of a goal-setting discussion is time management. For example, suppose a student sets a short-term goal of making an A on the weekly spelling test. He may be a poor speller and, in fact, go to special classes for students with language deficits. This student may also tend to procrastinate when it comes to studying. Designing a time management system that has the student study six words right after dinner each night Monday through Wednesday with a review of the words Thursday night and Friday morning can help this student reach his goal.

Students should become aware of how they spend their time by completing charts that outline what they do every hour of the day. It can be enlightening for students to realize that they spend four hours a day watching television. A book report assignment is a good time to discuss time management in class and help students decide how many pages they should read a day and at what time of the day they should read to complete the book on time. Making long-term assignments and helping the students divide the assignment into more manageable units can help them become organized and more systematic in their study.

UNDERSTANDING LEARNING PREFERENCES

> *Byron consistently made Ds on his weekly spelling tests, although he insisted that he studied every night, following the time schedule he and his teacher had designed. Upon further discussion, Byron's teacher found that he was studying the spelling words orally. Byron's teacher explained to him that people generally learn in three different ways: visually (seeing), auditorily (hearing), or by a hands-on approach (doing or writing).*
>
> *When Byron learned how to write and rewrite the spelling word while studying with his father, he seemed to remember the correct spellings longer and perform better on tests.*

The three modalities—visual, auditory, and kinesthetic—are considered so important that a deficit in one of these areas can be a basis for placing a student in special education classes. Students who recognize which combinations of modalities they use to learn can become even more efficient in their study; teachers can help students use the area that will help them learn best.

Many adults seem to have figured out how they learn best. Visual learners like to read a book or see a film. These learners are the students who are unable to remember much lecture information but rely heavily on reading the textbook. Auditory learners prefer to listen to lectures and learn through discussions. Kinesthetic learners seem to learn best by doing. These type of learners take lots of notes—some they never look at again, but they know that the act of writing the notes will help them learn the information. Activities and discussions that help students learn more about learning preferences have two purposes: (1) to help them understand there are different ways to learn and (2) to help them decide which modality to use at different times.

Once Byron was aware that he was not learning his spelling words by orally spelling them, he was able to adjust his study pattern to include writing the words. Involving his motor skills improved his learning. Other students, especially students who lack a fluent handwriting system, are just the opposite—writing the words actually slows down their learning.

SUMMARY

Students need to learn organizational skills—from keeping a neat desk, work folder, and assignment sheet to scheduling an appropriate time and place to study. Unit booklets also help students organize and integrate their study. Students should also become aware of the learning styles and how to maximize use of their preferred learning style for more effective learning.

SUGGESTED CLASSROOM ACTIVITIES

═══ GOALS ═══

1. *Organize student desks.*
2. *Begin to use a work folder.*
3. *Begin to use an assignment sheet.*
4. *Increase awareness of appropriate home study skills.*
5. *Use scheduling/goal-setting techniques.*
6. *Increase awareness of learning styles.*

Week 2

Desk/Work Folder/Assignment Sheet

1. Review the study skills discussed from last week (active reading, active listening, looking for new words, asking questions, trying hard). Introduce the pyramid style of desk organization and have all students organize their desks in this manner. Have the students draw a picture of a desk organized in this way and add it to their Study Skills Notebook.

2. Now that their desks are neatly organized, students will need a place to file papers that are not yet finished and those that are complete but have not been collected. Hand out a work folder with two pockets and clips for paper. Explain that this system is much like any filing system that offices maintain. In the middle of the work folder, students should place an assignment sheet. This sheet should be filled out daily and assignments crossed off as completed.

3. Periodically, check desks, work folders, and assignment sheets. Give some type of reward to those who have kept up with all three areas. For students who require extra monitoring to finish work and turn it in, the following is recommended:
   a. Teachers should initial assignment pads daily before the students leave for the day.
   b. Parents should initial their child's assignment pad daily.
   c. If the student does not get the teacher or parent to initial the pad, loss of play time, television time, or other negative consequence should result. Likewise, students who do get their pads initialed should receive some small reward.

4. Some students will need to use a Friday System (see Student Activity 4) to help ensure that work is completed, is turned in, and is of good quality. Each Friday, the teacher fills out a Friday Sheet for students who require extra monitoring. Weekly grades are recorded, along with any

missing work and teacher comments. Each Friday, the parents should look for this paper and give appropriate rewards and consequences. Teachers can use the Friday System for students who require more structure and need to have their parents informed about their progress weekly.

Studying at Home/Scheduling

As a class, brainstorm some of the worst places to study and state the reason why these places are not conducive to productive study. For example:

Worst Place to Study	Why
Subway	Noisy, moving, no supplies
At Putt-Putt Golf	Distracting, noisy

Pass out Student Activity 5, *Places to Study*. Have the students fill out this handout, share their ideas with a partner, and then share ideas as a whole class (Think-Pair-Share). Students should add this paper to the Study Skills Notebook.

Goal Setting and Schedules

1. Read a book, such as *The Little Engine That Could* (or other applicable book), and discuss the need for setting goals. Discuss a personal goal and how people achieve their goals.

2. Have students complete Student Activity 6, *Long-Term Goals*, share their papers in small groups, and then file them in the Study Skills Notebook. Explain that these are all long-term goals. Choose several of these goals and brainstorm how these goals can be achieved. For example:

Goal	How
Veterinarian	Go to school, study hard
Soccer player	Practice, join a team

3. Give all students a copy of Student Activity 7, *Goals for This Week*. Have them decide on three short-term goals for the week, such as getting an A on a spelling test, reading 10 pages a day in a book, and so on. At the end of the day, have the students fill out the checklist for that day and review their goals. Continue to do this each afternoon for the rest of the week. File this sheet in the Study Skills Notebook. Use this handout periodically to improve self-monitoring skills and increase awareness of goal-setting skills.

4. Pass out Student Activity 8, *General Assignment Sheet*, or Student Activity 9, *Assignment Pad by Class*. Go over this handout as a class. Discuss the importance of writing down assignments.

5. If you give long-term assignments, then give each student weekly or monthly calendars to fill out and use for scheduling time to work on

projects. Student Activities 10, *Weekly Calendar*, and 11, *Monthly Calendar*, may provide structure for students.

Doing Homework

1. Ask students to guess how much time they spend a week at school, at recreational activity (such as ballet, baseball, watching television), and at doing homework. Then give each student a copy of Student Activity 12, *How You Spend Your Time*, to fill out according to their own individual schedules. Let them figure out the actual time spent in each activity and compare to their previous guess.

2. Discuss the letter to parents, entitled *Homework*, with students (Student Activity 13) and then send it home.

3. Discuss Student Activity 14, *Hints for Homework*, with students. This activity is designed to help students make the most of their homework time. This should be filed in their Study Skills Notebooks.

Learning Preferences

1. Introduce students to the idea of three learning styles. Explain that most people prefer to learn using one of the three ways: visual (looking), auditory (listening), kinesthetic (writing, doing).

2. In small groups, have students fill out individual copies of Student Activity 15, *Ways We Learn*. Share ideas as a large group by making a class chart such as this:

Seeing	Listening	Doing
Movies	Radio	Eating
Reading	Lectures	Puzzles
TV	Tapes	Models
Photographs	Music	Cooking
		Baseball

Unit Booklets

Help students to organize information sequentially by subject by requiring unit booklets such as the one they are keeping now for this study skills unit. Materials for a unit of study, such as the four food groups, should be kept in a booklet with a table of contents. New material should be added as the unit of study progresses.

Name _____ Date _____

STUDENT ACTIVITY 4

FRIDAY SYSTEM

On the next page are the grades you have earned this week in each class, as filled out by your teachers. Take this home and have your parent sign it.

1. Are all your test and quiz grades good? _____

   _____

2. Which grades do you want to improve next week? _____

   _____

   _____

3. What will you do to improve your grades for next week? _____

   _____

4. If you have any missing work, what can you do to be sure this does not happen again? _____

   _____

   _____

5. Has your conduct been good? _____ If not, what can you do to improve in this area? _____

   _____

   _____

Class	Test grades	Quizzes	Homework grades	Missing work	Conduct	Comments	Initials Teacher/Parent

Name _____   Date _____

STUDENT ACTIVITY 5

PLACES TO STUDY

1. Think about the worst place to study at your house. Write a paragraph about this place. Explain why it is such a bad place to study. Draw a picture on another piece of paper to go with your paragraph.

_____

_____

_____

_____

_____

_____

2. Think about the best place to study at your house. Write a paragraph about this place. Explain why it is such a good place to study. Draw a picture on another piece of paper to go with your paragraph.

_____

_____

_____

_____

_____

_____

Name _____   Date _____

STUDENT ACTIVITY 6

LONG-TERM GOALS

Describe yourself in 20 years, including where you will live, what you will do for a job, what your house will be like, and the people/animals you live with. Draw a picture of your house and other important things in your life.

_____

_____

_____

_____

_____

_____

_____

Name _____ Date _____

STUDENT ACTIVITY 7

GOALS FOR THIS WEEK

Choose three goals for the week and write them here.

1. _____

2. _____

3. _____

Each day place a check in the box if you did what the sentence said.

	Monday	Tuesday	Wednesday	Thursday	Friday
I was an active reader.					
I was an active listener.					
I asked questions.					
I learned new words.					
I tried hard.					
I kept my desk clean and orderly, with books stacked in a pyramid.					
I kept a list of assignments.					
I kept a work folder.					
I worked to achieve my goals.					

Did you reach your goals? Explain here.

1. _____

2. _____

3. _____

Name _____ Date _____

STUDENT ACTIVITY 8

GENERAL ASSIGNMENT SHEET

Write down all daily assignments. Have your teacher and parent sign this sheet daily.

Week of _____   My Goal_____

Monday

_____

_____

_____

_____

Teacher's initials _____ Parent's initials _____

Tuesday

_____

_____

_____

_____

Teacher's initials _____ Parent's initials _____

(continued)

Wednesday

_____

_____

_____

_____

Teacher's initials _____ Parent's initials _____

Thursday

_____

_____

_____

_____

Teacher's initials _____ Parent's initials _____

Friday

_____

_____

_____

_____

Teacher's initials _____ Parent's initials _____

Have I met my goal?   YES_____   NO_____

Name _____ Date _____

STUDENT ACTIVITY 9

ASSIGNMENT PAD BY CLASS

On the following sheet, write down all daily assignments. Have your teacher and parent sign this sheet daily.

Week of _____

1. My short-term goals for the week are:

    a. _____

    b. _____

    c. _____

2. At the end of this week, answer the following questions:

    a. Did you meet all of your goals? _____

    b. If not, what can you do next week to be sure you meet these goals? _____

    _____

    _____

    _____

    _____

    _____

    _____

(continued)

Monday

Reading _____

Spelling _____

Vocab. _____

Math _____

Science _____

Soc. St. _____

Other _____

Teacher/Parent _____

Initials _____

Tuesday

Reading _____

Spelling _____

Vocab. _____

Math _____

Science _____

Soc. St. _____

Other _____

Teacher/Parent _____

Initials _____

Wednesday

Reading _____

Spelling _____

Vocab. _____

Math _____

Science _____

Soc. St. _____

Other _____

Teacher/Parent _____

Initials _____

Thursday

Reading _____

Spelling _____

Vocab. _____

Math _____

Science _____

Soc. St. _____

Other _____

Teacher/Parent _____

Initials _____

Friday

Reading _____

Spelling _____

Vocab. _____

Math _____

Science _____

Soc. St. _____

Other _____

Teacher/Parent _____

Initials _____

Name _____   Date _____

STUDENT ACTIVITY 10

WEEKLY CALENDAR

Block off time to study each day.

	Monday	Tuesday	Wednesday	Thursday	Friday	Saturday	Sunday
7:00 to 8:00							
8:00 to 9:00							
9:00 to 10:00							
10:00 to 11:00							
11:00 to 12:00							
12:00 to 1:00							
1:00 to 2:00							
2:00 to 3:00							
3:00 to 4:00							
4:00 to 5:00							
5:00 to 6:00							
6:00 to 7:00							
7:00 to 8:00							
8:00 to 9:00							

Name _____ Date _____

STUDENT ACTIVITY 11

MONTHLY CALENDAR

Using the calendar on the next page, complete the following;

1. Write the date for each day of the month in the little boxes.

2. Write down when each assignment is due.

3. Write down what you will do on each day to be sure that all work is done on time.

4. At the end of the month, check over your calendar. Were all assignments done on time? _____

   If not, what can you do next month to be sure that all work is done on time?

   _____

   _____

   _____

   _____

   _____

   _____

   _____

   _____

Sunday	Monday	Tuesday	Wednesday	Thursday	Friday	Saturday

Name _____   Date _____

STUDENT ACTIVITY 12

HOW YOU SPEND YOUR TIME

Decide how many hours per week you think you spend on each of the activities:

_____ hours a week at school

_____ hours a week in recreational activities

_____ hours a week in watching television

_____ hours a week doing homework.

Now fill out the chart on the next page. For example, if you are in school from 8:00 to 3:00, write "school" at the 8:00 slot and block off this time until 3:00. Count the hours from 8:00 to 3:00 and multiply by 5 days to get how many hours a week you spend in school. Continue in this way to figure out how you spend your week, then write the hours below.

I *actually* spend

_____ hours a week at school

_____ hours a week in recreational activities

_____ hours a week watching television

_____ hours a week doing homework

How close were your guesses?

	Sunday	Monday	Tuesday	Wednesday	Thursday	Friday	Saturday
6:00							
7:00							
8:00							
9:00							
10:00							
11:00							
12:00							
1:00							
2:00							
3:00							
4:00							
5:00							
6:00							
7:00							
8:00							
9:00							

Name _____   Date _____

STUDENT ACTIVITY 13

HOMEWORK

Dear Parents,

This year your child will be responsible for homework. He or she has been taught during class to:

- Read actively
- Listen actively
- Look for new words
- Ask questions
- Try hard

Your son or daughter has also been instructed to keep a/an:

- clean, organized desk
- work folder
- assignment sheet or pad

If you are unsure what homework, projects, book reports, and tests your child has been assigned, this information should be found on his or her assignment sheet. *I need your help.* At home, please help your child with the following:

1. Find a quiet place to study.
2. Gather all necessary supplies such as paper, pencils, and a dictionary.
3. Decide on a definite time each day to study.
4. Encourage taking 5-minute breaks every 20 to 30 minutes.
5. As assignments are completed, they should be marked off the assignment pad.
6. Divide book reports and other long projects into units of work to be completed each night. (For example, a 100-page book report due in 11 days results in 10 days' reading each night with one night to write the report.)
7. Review notes and chapters in science and social studies even when there is not a test the next day.
8. Read to your child (books, magazines, recipes, jokes, instructional manuals, etc.).

Name _____ Date _____

STUDENT ACTIVITY 14

HINTS FOR HOMEWORK

I. Place

   A. Find a quiet place to study, free from distractions.

   B. Have all necessary supplies (pencils, dictionary, paper, etc.).

II. Schedule

   A. Decide on a definite time to study (such as right after school or after dinner).

   B. Every 20 to 30 minutes take a short break (adjust this time according to your activity level).

   C. If spelling is especially hard for you, try dividing the words into groups. Learn Group 1 on Monday, review Group 1 on Tuesday and learn Group 2 on Tuesday, and so on.

   D. Divide book reports and projects into manageable units. For example, if a 50-page book report is due in six days, then read each night and spend the last night used to write the report.

III. Studying for spelling tests

   A. Look for patterns (do all words have one certain vowel pattern?)

   B. Divide long words into syllables (au to bi og ra phy).

   C. Write a spelling word on the top of a piece of paper.

      1. Look at the word.

      2. Spell the word out loud.

      3. Fold the paper to cover up the spelling word.

      4. Write the word again, but this time from memory.

      5. Open the paper and compare the spelling word with the way you wrote it the first time. Did you spell it correctly?

Name _____   Date _____

STUDENT ACTIVITY 15

WAYS WE LEARN

We learn about our world in three ways: visually (seeing), auditorily (listening), and kinesthetically (doing, writing). Some people learn best by reading a chapter (seeing), others by listening to lectures (listening), and others by writing notes (doing). Complete the exercise below.

List things you learn about by seeing.

_____

_____

_____

_____

List things you learn about by listening.

_____

_____

_____

_____

List things you learn about by doing or writing.

_____

_____

_____

_____

I believe I learn best by _____.

Chapter

4

Preparing Students to Read

Overview

Readers who take a few minutes to prepare themselves to read can save themselves time because these activities lead to improved comprehension. Awareness of text structure, both narrative and expository, can help students identify and remember main ideas and adjust their rate of reading. Scanning for and understanding key words can facilitate successful reading and remembering.

Fourth-grade students Meredith and Molly were spending the afternoon together and reading a section in their science book for the next day. After about five minutes of reading, Meredith looked up and noticed that Molly was still flipping pages of the book and making notes. Meredith reminded Molly that if she did not start reading soon, they would have no time to play.

Molly, however, was really saving time. She was making decisions about type of text, how fast to read, and her purpose for reading. She jotted down notes about what she knew and what questions she had about the subject, including any new or key words. After explaining her prereading strategy to Meredith, Molly explained, "It is better to read right *rather than to read over and over again."*

Teachers generally have two goals during instruction: to have students learn some particular body of information and to teach strategies to help students learn for themselves. The goal of study skills instruction is to foster independent learning (Dupuis, Lee, Badiali, & Askov, 1989). If students have learned to make the most of their initial study, they will remember more of what they read and be able to apply this new knowledge more effectively.

Previewing text helps readers know what information deserves their attention. Efficient readers direct their attention to the important ideas (Anderson & Pearson, 1984). Making decisions about type of text, rate and purpose of reading, knowledge of key vocabulary, and amount of prior knowledge of the subject facilitates deeper processing of the information being read. This previewing of text may take a few minutes prior to reading, but these minutes are well spent because this activity helps the reader connect new information to what is already known.

In this chapter, we will present ways to prepare students to read most effectively. The features of narrative and expository text, remembering main ideas, identifying and learning key words, and flexible reading rate will be discussed.

KINDS OF TEXT

Students know that a social studies textbook looks different from a storybook, and even young students can make a prediction about what will happen next in a story because they know, generally, how stories "go." Before studying, a student must think about the structure of the text, so that more accurate predictions can be made about content.

Text structure refers to how the author organizes ideas in a particular text. Over time and through exposure, readers gradually become familiar with the general structures of written texts and develop a schema for text structure (Harris & Sipay, 1990). Students have a sense of narrative text structure before they enter school because they have already been exposed to stories for years. Awareness of expository text, however, begins about third grade (Gillis & Olson, 1987), perhaps because of the frequency of exposure to this type of text.

When students are sensitive to text structure, they tend to remember what they read more accurately and over a longer period of time (Taylor, 1982). However, teachers often fail to devote any time to helping students learn to be sensitive to text structure. Awareness of text structure is an important metacognitive skill that should be made a part of learning to read and write. Generally, two types of text are found in school settings: narrative and expository.

Narrative text is usually encountered in stories commonly found in basal readers. Narrative text generally relates to a series of events that are related to each other, and usually has the following elements: setting, sequence, characterization, and plot. A reader can expect meeting characters, a time period and a setting, a series of events, and some sort of resolution. Story maps can help heighten student awareness of the structure of stories. Story maps facilitate the identification of the different predictable aspects of a story.

Some teachers find it helpful to show students a story map before the reading. Then, as stories are read aloud, students note the structure and seem better able to understand the story and the structure as a result of this exercise. Shown here is a story map of the "Three Little Pigs."

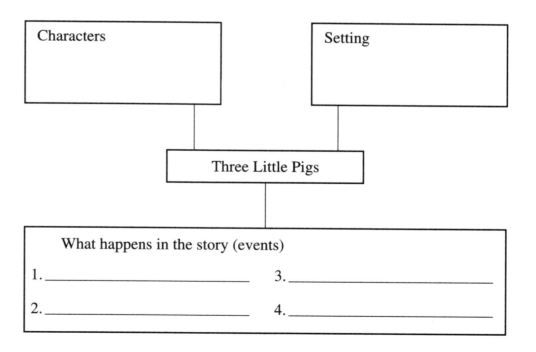

Story maps may be modified to fit different purposes. Students can fill in the different parts of the map as a teacher reads a story to them. This diagram can then be used as a springboard for discussion. Students can be asked to read the story first and then fill in the story structure.

Expository text is the type of writing typically found in social studies or science textbooks. This type of writing provides an explanation of facts and concepts, and a reader can usually identify a hierarchy of ideas. Students at all levels tend not to be very skilled in using text structure to improve comprehension (McGee, 1982).

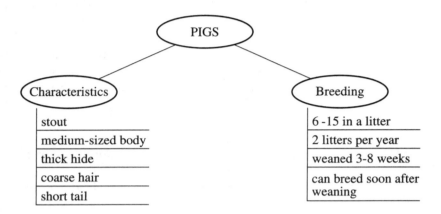

"Elementary and secondary school students who have been taught to identify the structure of expository and narrative text have been found to have better comprehension than students who have not received much instruction" in text structure (Taylor, 1992, p. 222). Competency in using text structure seems to facilitate comprehension and seems to improve with age and ability (Harris & Sipay, 1990). Primary-grade instruction should focus on an awareness of the two types of text, whereas intermediate-level instruction can contain a more sophisticated emphasis on the different types of expository text and the signal words that cue a reader to text structure. Sensitivity to text structure naturally leads to understanding how to use the adjunct aids that writers employ to accentuate the important ideas in the text.

IDENTIFYING AND REMEMBERING MAIN IDEAS

Many elementary students have difficulty reading for main ideas in their content area textbooks (Bauman, 1981; B. M. Taylor, 1980; K. K. Taylor, 1986; Winograd, 1984), which is a skill that depends on the sensitivity to text structure. Also, poorer readers have difficulty stating the main ideas in expository text (Winograd & Bridge, 1986).

Writers accentuate important ideas in text by using adjunct aids. Parts of the textbook (questions and activities), typographical aids (headings, subheadings, and marked words), pictorial aids (pictures, illustrations, diagrams, maps, tables, and graphs), glossaries, introductions, and summaries are devices that are designed to draw the reader's attention to important ideas in the text. Comprehension can be improved by direct instruction in the use of these adjunct aids.

Key words, essential to the understanding of the text, are usually marked in boldface type or italics. Comprehension can be improved if students take the time to decide if these key words are familiar to them and find out more about them before reading. Key words are usually key concepts necessary to understand the reading.

KEY WORDS

Dale, a fifth-grade remedial reading student, excitedly entered his reading class Tuesday morning. Tuesdays were D.E.A.R. time (Drop Everything And Read). During D.E.A.R. time, students read selections of their choice silently, in pairs, and to the teacher. Dale had checked out The Flounder in the Sea *from the school library and had practiced reading it the night before. Aware that he had a "reading problem," he was excited about showing his teacher that he could read this book by himself.*

When Dale's turn came, he read his story fluently to his very pleased teacher. When he finished the story, his teacher began to discuss the story with Dale, probing to see if he understood the story. During the discussion, Dale's teacher surmised that something was missing from his understanding. Deciding to start with what he thought was an easy question, the teacher asked, "What is a flounder?" Dale smiled and said, "I don't know."

Dale had read the entire story and did not understand the key word and not once had he stopped to ask. How could he possibly understand the story?

A person can read a narrative passage with every *sixth* word being unfamiliar if they have good contextual analysis and morphemic analysis skills. That is, a reader can understand text by guessing at the meaning of every sixth word (Nagy, 1988). The important difference between this research finding and Dale's dilemma is *key words*. If the word is important to the understanding of the story, as was *flounder*, students must take the time to figure out the meaning. If Dale would have guessed that a flounder was "some kind of fish that lives on the bottom of the sea" or even "some kind of fish," he would have understood the story. As it was, Dale was concentrating more on pronouncing the words correctly than understanding the role of one of the main characters in the story.

It is of little value to read an expository passage or story without understanding the key words. Students who read in this way are not strategic readers and will not gain meaning from print. Breaking students of this habit of just reading words can be difficult. One of the most effective ways is to model the process. Demonstrate to the students that when you come across a word you do not understand, you find the meaning by first trying to figure out the meaning of the word from context or through morphemic analysis. If that is not enough, you may ask someone or consult a dictionary.

Students should be encouraged to look for unfamiliar words while surveying a passage. They should be praised for asking what unfamiliar words mean. Often teacher's manuals will contain a list of new vocabulary words. Prereading strategies using key words can increase motivation to read and facilitate a successful reading experience.

Strategic readers understand what they read and understand that they cannot comprehend the passage if they do not comprehend key words. Teachers can help students actively look for unfamiliar words and guess at their meaning from context. Strategic readers also know that some texts take more prereading activity, some texts require more attention to key words, and it is advisable to read some text more slowly than others.

FLEXIBLE READING

Efficient reading is "flexible." Students should be able to adjust their rate according to their purpose for reading, their prior knowledge, and the nature of the material.*

For example, consider two students: Alesha and Anna. The physical education teacher has given them a small book on soccer and tells them that they will have a test on Friday that will cover soccer rules. Alesha has been playing soccer on city teams since she was 6 years old, and her mother is a soccer coach. Therefore, often the game is dinner-time conversation. Anna, on the other hand, has taken violin lessons since age 6, her father is a chemist, and she has never played a game of soccer. Alesha needs only to skim the material, stopping periodically and checking to make sure her prior knowledge of the rules match the text. She reads the book rapidly and hurries off to a match. Anna, however, spends hours with the book, writing down the rules so that she can study them later, and she asks Alesha the meaning of such terms as *off-sides* and *heading*. Good readers decide how fast to read before beginning and adjust their rate while reading according to their comprehension.

The ability to read quickly pays off for college students and professionals. But "reading" text quickly without understanding is a waste of time. On the other hand, reading slowly and carefully may be inefficient as well. So how fast should a person read? The answer depends on the purpose for reading (including knowledge of the criterion task), the reader's prior knowledge, and the nature of the material. Reading speed also fluctuates with grade level (ability), although the relationship between reading speed and comprehension changes dramatically as children's reading abilities develop.

It is not appropriate to push elementary children who are in the process of learning to read to read faster. This could be detrimental to

*This and the next paragraph are from *Reading and the Middle School Student: Strategies to Enhance Literacy* by Judith L. Irvin, 1990, Boston: Allyn and Bacon. Reprinted by permission.

children who have not become proficient at rapid word recognition. It is difficult to try to read fast when one cannot yet recognize words quickly. However, it is most appropriate that elementary-age students learn the different reasons for reading and the different reading rates that pertain to those reasons for reading.

Study rate is the slowest rate but results in the greatest comprehension. This rate is appropriate for content material. *Average rate* is faster but results in less comprehension. Stories are read at this rate. *Fast rate* is used when skimming and scanning. With this knowledge and teacher encouragement, students can begin to adjust their speed according to their purpose for reading.

Fifth-grade students can begin to practice pleasure reading at a quicker pace by using materials that are easy for them to read. Poor readers and students with learning disabilities should not practice increasing their rate by using grade-level textbooks. Reading material should be at least a full grade level below their instructional level. Instruction in increased rate should be informal and nonstressful. Some teachers have found a game format, such as Beat the Clock, helpful in increasing reading rate.

SUMMARY

Efficient readers read text right the first time rather than over and over. *Right reading* includes awareness of text structure—both narrative and expository—and making decisions about how to proceed with the reading task. Efficient readers also adjust their reading rate to the type of text and the task at hand. Right reading also includes scanning for and understanding key words that may be important in reading the text. Although right reading takes some time before reading, it saves time in the long run when these activities lead to improved comprehension of text.

SUGGESTED CLASSROOM ACTIVITIES

═══ GOALS ═══

1. Understand text structure (narrative and expository).

2. Understand book parts.

3. Understand paragraph structure.

4. Use flexible reading rates.

Week 3

1. Have students take out their Study Skills Notebooks and fill out the *Study Skills Review 1* (Student Activity 16) independently. After a class review, file the sheet in the notebooks.

   Answer Key for Student Activity 16:

1. actively	8. assignment
2. listen	9. quiet
3. meanings	10. (answers will vary) pencils, dictionary
4. questions	11. break
5. try	12. (answers will vary)
6. pyramid	13. visual, auditory, kinesthetic (or doing)
7. work	14. (answers will vary)

2. On Monday, at the end of the day, give each student a copy of *Goals for This Week* (Student Activity 7) from last week to fill out each afternoon.

3. Explain that this week they will learn more about being active readers. Divide the class into groups of about five students each. Place textbooks that are both narrative (stories) and expository (science and social studies) with each group. Ask the group to divide the books into two categories—do not tell students which types of categories. Let the students discuss and share their choices. Respecting all choices, explain that books can be divided into two categories: narrative and expository. Explain these terms and divide the books accordingly. Have students explain why they put books into each category.

4. Pass out *Two Types of Text* (Student Activity 17). Have students fill these out individually and share as a group. Guide the class into beginning to think about three different reading rates. (File the handout in the Study Skills Notebooks.)

5. Using a content book, discuss important book parts that can help students read actively (quickly and accurately) and learn new words.

Point out book parts such as a title, a subtitle, an index, and a glossary. Discuss why each book part can be helpful to a reader.

6. Pass out *Book Scavenger Hunt* (Student Activity 18) and instruct students to use this handout with a expository book that you have chosen. Have students share their answers in a small group. In pairs, let the students make up book scavenger hunts for each other.

7. Make a group chart of book parts that are helpful as a class. Be sure to include the table of contents, index, glossary, boldface type, pictures, charts, titles, and subtitles.

8. Pass out *Paragraph Structure* (Student Activity 19). Go over the five different types of paragraph structure on the board, then have students complete the sheet. File the handout in the Study Skills Notebooks.

Answer Key for Student Activity 19:

1. ▽ Main idea first

2. ☐ No main idea

3. ⬦ Main idea in the middle (she had hit her first homerun).

4. △ Main idea last

5. ✕ Main idea at the beginning and the end

9. Using *Paragraph Structure in Expository Text* (Student Activity 20), go through the first two paragraphs together as a class. Have students highlight the main idea. After each paragraph, decide what structure it has and draw the shape out to the side. After doing the first two paragraphs together, let students do the next paragraphs independently but share and discuss their answers with others immediately after each paragraph is finished. File the handout in the Study Skills Notebooks.

Answer Key for Student Activity 20:

1. ✕ First two sentences and last sentence

2. ▽ First sentence

3. ▽ First sentence

4. ▽ First sentence

5. △ Last sentence

10. Have students complete *Paragraph Structure—Writing Your Own* (Student Activity 21) individually and then share in groups. This activity may need teacher guidance. Be sure the main idea is not at the beginning in both paragraphs.

11. Periodically discuss paragraph structure when reading science, social studies, and other books.

12. Discuss and complete *Paragraph Purpose* (Student Activity 22) with students. File the handout in the Study Skills Notebooks.

    Answer Key for Student Activity 22:

    1. Get your interest
    2. Main idea
    3. Fact
    4. Fact
    5. Fact
    6. Fact
    7. Fact
    8. Get your interest

13. On Friday have students complete and review Student Activity 7 (started on Monday). Check to see if the students reached their goals. File the handout in the Study Skills Notebooks.

14. Explain the three different reading rates using Student Activity 23, *Reading Rate—An Analogy*. Have the students fill out and share the bottom part of this paper. File the handout in the Study Skills Notebooks. During the next weeks, ask students at what rate they should read certain books.

    Answer Key for Student Activity 23:

    1. Study rate—Mollie
    2. Average rate—Kyle
    3. Fast rate—Dan

15. Use Student Activity 24, *Key Words*, to discuss with students the importance of finding the meanings of key words.

    Answer Key for Student Activity 24:

    a. poggy = small, clear pond
    b. loated = scared
    c. muf = bad

Name _____   Date _____

STUDENT ACTIVITY 16

STUDY SKILLS REVIEW 1

Fill in the blanks below using the information you have learned about study skills. The first one is done for you.

1. I read _____*actively*_____.

2. I _____ actively.

3. I find the _____ of new words.

4. I ask _____.

5. I _____ hard.

6. My desk is organized in a _____ form.

7. I file classwork and homework sheets in my _____ folder.

8. I keep an _____ sheet filled out.

9. At home I study in a _____ place.

10. I gather all supplies when I study, such as _____ ,

    _____ , and_____.

11. I take a study _____ every 20 to 30 minutes.

12. The best time for me to study at home is_____.

13. The three learning styles are _____ ,

    _____ , and_____.

14. I think I can learn best by_____.

Name _____   Date _____

TWO TYPES OF TEXT

The two types of books are narrative and expository. Narrative text tells a story, such as "The Three Little Pigs." Expository text teaches facts and concepts, such as a science book. Complete the exercise below.

1. List five books under each category.

   Narrative

   a. _____

   b. _____

   c. _____

   d. _____

   e. _____

   Expository

   a. _____

   b. _____

   c. _____

   d. _____

   e. _____

2. Place an *S* next to the books you would read slowly and carefully. Place an *F* next to the books you would read fairly fast.

Name _____ Date _____

STUDENT ACTIVITY 18

BOOK SCAVENGER HUNT

Choose an expository book and answer these questions.

1. What is the title of your book? _____

2. Who is the author? _____

3. What date was the book published? _____

4. What is the title of the first chapter or story?

    _____

5. On what page does the fourth chapter begin? _____

6. Read through the chapters in the Table of Contents quickly and write down the name of one chapter that sounds interesting.

    _____

7. Find a subtitle anywhere in the book. Write down the subtitle and the page you found it on. Page _____

    Subtitle _____

8. What book part is found at the end of your book? _____

    _____

9. Does your book use underlining or boldface type?   YES   NO

10. Find a chart or graph in your book. Write the page number you found it on. Page _____

11. Do you think this book has some interesting ideas?   YES   NO

12. Find four new words and list them below:

    _____   _____

    _____   _____

Name _____   Date _____

STUDENT ACTIVITY 19

PARAGRAPH STRUCTURE

Following are the five common paragraph shapes:

Main idea ▽ Details	□ Details	Details △ Main idea	Details ◇ Main idea Details ◇ Main idea	Main idea ✕ Details Main idea

Read the following paragraphs. Underline the main idea and draw the shape in the right column.

Paragraph Shapes

1. If I were in charge of the world, I would be rich. I would buy toys and animals and a big red car. I would also live in a beautiful mansion.

2. I have black hair that I tie back with a yellow ribbon. My eyes are brown and my nose is just the right size for me.

3. Keri ran home from school. She could hardly contain her excitement. Finally, after weeks of practice, she had hit her first homerun. Keri could hardly wait to tell her mom all about it.

4. The clouds were getting dark and the lightning flashed across the sky. People went searching for their umbrellas. It was about to rain.

5. Missy the cat was Bucky's worst enemy. Bucky was sitting on the couch when he heard Missy. Missy was outside Bucky's front door meowing on "his" front steps. Bucky sprang to his feet and raced to the front door barking. He scratched at the door for several minutes. Finally, giving up, Bucky sat by the door and whined. Bucky hated Missy.

Name _____ Date _____

STUDENT ACTIVITY 20

PARAGRAPH STRUCTURE IN EXPOSITORY TEXT

Read and underline the main idea. Then draw the paragraph shape out to the side.

THE POND MAYFLY

A pond looks like a tranquil place. But it is not. There is a constant struggle for life under the pond's calm and peaceful surface. The struggle goes on among the stems of plants, in the shade of floating leaves and in the mud at the bottom. Chase and escape, eating and being eaten—this is the true life of the pond.

One of the best known dwellers of a pond is the mayfly. One pond will contain thousands of mayflies. They are food for other animals in and near the pond. In their first stage of life, mayflies live in water. They are flat, small insects. They have thin gills that wave quickly on the sides of their stomachs. The mayfly is noted for this movement.

Mayfly young can't protect themselves from enemies. They hide where they can in the pond. They cling to the leaves of twigs. They crawl into the sand on the bottom to keep from being seen.

A mayfly is fully grown after a whole year. Then it is ready to leave the pond. It slowly rises to the surface of the water. Here a great change takes place. The skin splits along the back. Out comes a fragile, winged adult with a small head, a thin body and two

Paragraph Shapes

(continued)

or three long tail fibers. It rests on the water for a short time. Then it rises from the surface in shaky flight.

Adult mayflies live for just a few hours, or at the most a few days. During this time they do not eat. They have no mouths with which to catch or eat food. Instead, they live on food stored in their bodies. In the short time that they have wings, the adults mate and lay their eggs. Then they die. Though it lives a short life, a mayfly is an important part of life in a pond.

The passage is from "The Pond Mayfly" in *Essential Skills: Book 1* by Walter Pauk. Copyright © 1982 by Jamestown Publishers, Providence, Rhode Island. Reprinted by permission.

Name _____ Date _____

STUDENT ACTIVITY 21

PARAGRAPH STRUCTURE— WRITING YOUR OWN

Organize the following information into two paragraphs on another sheet of paper. Write one paragraph with the main idea first and the other paragraph with the main idea last or in the middle.

THE TASMANIAN DEVIL

Characteristics
12 to 20 pounds
Very strong
Large head
Black fur
White patches
Stout
Looks like a small bear

Hunter
Savage attacker
Kills in seconds
Eats dead or living flesh
Can kill large or small animals

Drawing used with permission of Turman Publishing Co., Seattle.

Name _____ Date _____

STUDENT ACTIVITY 22

PARAGRAPH PURPOSE

Paragraphs are generally written with one of three purposes:

1. Get your interest.
2. Give main ideas.
3. Give facts.

Read the following passage and decide the purpose for each paragraph. Write the purpose out to the side. The first one is done for you.

THE CUCKOO

When someone is acting extremely oddly, we say that a person is "cuckoo." The word comes from the cuckoo bird, which lives in many parts of the world. The cuckoo does do some rather peculiar things, but it's really not fair to say the cuckoo is "cuckoo." Any animal that can trick another creature into raising its young has to be pretty smart.

Get your interest
_____

That's exactly what many species of cuckoos do. They deposit their eggs in another bird's nest, then fly away, leaving the foster or host parents to sit on the egg and care for the baby bird when it hatches. The cuckoo chooses birds such as the magpie, warbler, sparrow, and even the tiny wren for this job.

_____

Other birds don't like cuckoos one bit. When they see cuckoos, they will often attack or "mob" them. But while one cuckoo is enduring the angry pecking, another cuckoo will sneak the egg into the nest in just a few seconds!

_____

Once the cuckoo egg is in the nest, the foster parents take care of it, even though it is often much bigger than their own eggs. When the cuckoo hatches, it is naked and blind. It spends the first days of its life trying to push everything, including any other eggs or chicks, out of the nest. Often it succeeds.

The young cuckoo is usually bigger than the other baby birds in the nest. Its huge mouth is always open, begging for more food even after it has been fed. The poor host parents must scurry to feed the ravenous freeloader, which frequently grows much bigger than they are! Sometimes the other baby birds don't get enough because the cuckoo is so greedy, and they die.

About three weeks after it hatches, the cuckoo is ready to fly off to find other cuckoos. Then it lives exactly like a cuckoo and eats one of its favorite foods, hairy caterpillars. Most other birds wouldn't even consider eating hairy caterpillars.

When the cuckoo is ready to lay eggs, it will look for a nest built by the same kind of birds that were its foster parents. When it finds such a nest, it deposits its eggs there.

Come to think of it, maybe some cuckoos are a bit "cuckoo." It is extremely odd that a cuckoo would think its mother is a tiny wren!

Passage and drawing are from *Amazing Animal Stories 4*. Copyright © 1981 Turman Publishing Co. Used with permission of Turman Publishing Co., Seattle.

(continued)

Name _____   Date _____

STUDENT ACTIVITY **23**

READING RATE—AN ANALOGY

WALKING	JOGGING	RACING
Study Rate	Average Rate	Fast Rate
Slow	Faster	Fastest
90% comprehension	70% comprehension	Main idea or detail
Textbook	**Novel**	**Dictionary**

Read the following story about three people looking at a forest. Compare these people to the reading rates. Decide which rate each person is using.

1. *Kyle* is jogging through the forest. It is Saturday and he loves to jog through the forest on Saturdays. He gets lots of exercise and fresh air. He enjoys looking at the trees as they seem to pass by him.

2. *Mollie* is a scientist. She is walking very slowly through the forest looking carefully at all the flowers, trees, and birds. She is also looking for small animals that live in the forest. Mollie needs to learn all about the forest because she is writing a book about forest life.

3. *Dan* has never seen a forest. He lives in New York in a big building. There are not many trees around his building. He cannot imagine what a forest looks like. In the summer, he visits his grandmother, who owns a small plane. Grandmother takes Dan for a ride in her plane. They fly quickly over a forest so Dan can get the idea of what a forest is.

Compare the different people in the forest with the different reading rates. Think about the different reasons they had for being in or above the forest. Complete the chart below.

Reading rates   *Person*

1. Study rate   _____

2. Average rate   _____

3. Fast rate   _____

Name _____ Date _____

STUDENT ACTIVITY 24

KEY WORDS

1. It is very important to look for new words as you read them and find their meanings. This can often be done by reading the sentences and figuring out the word meanings. Each of the following sentences has a nonsense word. Figure out the meaning for the nonsense word by reading the whole sentence. Finding the meanings of new words is like unlocking a riddle.

   a. As the early morning sun began to shine, the *poggy*, a small clear pond, became alive with water bugs.

      The meaning of *poggy* is _____ .

   b. Nancy thought that she would feel *loated* as the doctor cut off her cast, but actually she found that she was not scared at all, but re-lieved.

      The meaning of *loated* is _____ .

   c. Dan was not surprised when he received a *muf* grade on his social studies test since he had not studied.

      The meaning of *muf* is _____ .

2. Now create your own nonsense words and use them in sentences. Be sure that your sentence explains the meaning of the nonsense words.

   a. _____

      _____

      _____

   b. _____

      _____

      _____

   c. _____

      _____

      _____

Chapter

5

Promoting Active Reading

Overview

Students understand what they read and hear only if they read or listen actively *and have control over their comprehension (metacognition). Active reading can be facilitated through strategies such as self-questioning, INSERT, highlighting, and SQ3R.*

Ginny was having a hard time concentrating on her reading. The book she had chosen for Silent Reading Time was about a puppy who came to live with a family. Ginny loved dogs. In fact, she had a puppy of her own until it was killed. Ginny chose this book because she thought it might make her feel better. She gave up reading and just flipped through the pages, looking at the pictures. Although Ginny was not concentrating on her reading, she was relating to the author's words in her own personal way.

When it came time to read her science book about machines, she was still thinking about her puppy. While her eyes scanned the pages, none of the author's ideas were integrated with her own ideas. After a time, Ginny realized that she was not really reading and she knew that she would eventually need to construct a semantic map on machines and take a test on the information.

She started over and began to read actively. She began to ask herself questions about what she was reading and monitor whether or not she was understanding the content. She knew that her science book was different in structure from her storybook and began to identify the main ideas of her reading. When she did not understand the reading, she went back over the reading, looked ahead for a clue, or tried to guess at the meaning of the text. Once Ginny decided to take charge of her reading, she became more actively involved and the text made more sense to her.

Metacognition is the ability to think about and monitor one's own comprehension while reading or listening. Metacognition involves understanding the task of reading or listening, making predictions about text structure, monitoring understanding, and making use of a bank of strategies to help understand text or speech. Ginny understood that she would eventually need to construct a semantic map about machines and recall the information on a test; she adjusted her reading to expository text; she knew she must pay attention more during reading; and she employed self-questioning and survey techniques to help her understand and remember her reading.

The term *metacognition* was coined in the 1970s and borrowed from cognitive psychologists. Between 1980 and 1987, more than 200 articles were written on metacognition and reading (Paris, Wasik, & van der Westhuizen, 1988). Research on metacognition and reading has focused on three aspects: (1) knowledge about the task of reading (what makes someone a good reader), (2) how readers regulate their thinking (self-appraisal and self-management) (Brown, 1978; Paris & Winograd, 1990), and (3) strategies that promote students' knowledge and control over their reading (Paris, Wasik, & Turner, 1991).

Understanding the concept of metacognition can assist teachers in helping students to become more strategic in their reading. Young and less skilled readers usually fail to regulate their learning strategically. But "fundamental strategies have been taught with good results to students who do not use them spontaneously" (Garner, 1992, p. 247). Another important aspect of metacognition includes the affect and motivational characteristics of thinking (Garner, 1992; Paris & Winograd, 1990)—that is, how students feel about themselves as learners and their ability to complete the task is important. In this chapter, strategies that promote active reading and develop metacognition will be described.

STRATEGIES TO PROMOTE ACTIVE READING*

Self-Questioning

Teaching students to engage in self-questioning before, during, and after reading has been found to improve comprehension ability (Andre & Anderson, 1978–79; Singer & Donlan, 1988). The reasons for this improved performance may be that students are forced to pause frequently, determine whether or not they understood the text, and decide what strategic action should be taken next. Proficient readers naturally perform these tasks when they monitor their comprehension.

Self-questioning leads the student to an active monitoring of the learning activity. It is critical that students be taught how to ask good questions. Teachers can model the process of asking good questions rather than simply using questions as an oral quiz. Students should be given the opportunity to practice and evaluate good questions as they read various content area paragraphs (Tei & Stewart, 1985). Self-questions can be content oriented or process oriented. *Content* questions focus on the content of the reading, such as "How do we get energy from fossil fuels?" *Process* questions encourage students to monitor and check their own comprehension, such as "Am I understanding this reading?" or "What will the author explain next?" (Davey, 1985, p. 26). The following are examples of content and process questions before, during, and after reading:

Prior to reading, students may ask themselves:

- What is the topic?

- What will I learn?

- What type of task will I be asked to complete (test, report)?

- Do I know enough to skim the material or should I read slowly and carefully, perhaps taking notes?

- What is the organization of the text?

- What signal words might help me understand the text?

- What might I learn about from this reading?

*Material on pages 74–76 is from *Reading and the Middle School Student: Strategies to Enhance Literacy* by Judith L. Irvin, 1990, Boston: Allyn and Bacon. Reprinted by permission.

During reading, students may ask themselves:

- Do I understand what I am reading?

- Do I know characters, setting, events (narrative text)?

- Do I know the main points and important details (expository text)?

- What did I just read (summary)?

- What will I learn about next?

After reading, students might ask themselves:

- Do I understand what I just read?

- What did I just learn?

- What will I do with this information now?

Davey (1985) suggested that students can learn self-questioning behaviors by cognitive modeling—that is, the teacher must "think aloud" and give personal responses to questions. The process may be carried out with pairs of students to help less able readers adopt a more metacognitive approach to reading. Typically, less able readers are passive, and self-questioning helps them to become more involved and active while reading.

Another activity that seems to motivate students to ask good questions about content is to let them make up questions for the test. Teachers can share the kinds of questions they might ask and then let students share their own questions. The purpose of such an activity is to facilitate a shift from teacher-generated questioning to student-generated questioning. Having these questions in mind while reading helps students focus on the major ideas in the reading and thus helps them remember the content.

Fitzgerald (1989) suggested pairing students for reading a passage. Each student reads the first section and writes questions about important points in the passage. The pairs continue until they finish the passage, and after exchanging papers for answering, discuss their answers. Self-questioning and making predictions lead to the all-important metacognitive skill of self-monitoring.

INSERT

Vaughn and Estes (1986) developed the simple procedure of INSERT (Interactive Notation System for Effective Reading and Thinking) to help students become more involved in their reading; it also helps the students make decisions as they read and clarify their own reading. The strategy consists of a marking system that records the students' reactions to what is being read. If marking in a book is a problem, simply supply students with strips of paper to place alongside the text with each student's name and page number on the top. The marking system is as follows:

✓   I understand

○   New information

❑   Confusing

▼   Important information

For example, students would mark a "❑" for confusing text. Teachers can help students through such passages with added concept building. The entire INSERT marking system should be introduced gradually.

Underlining/Highlighting

Underlining/highlighting is one of the most popular aids used to study text. This study strategy requires that students know what is worth underlining or remembering. The major benefit of this study strategy comes not from merely marking information but from rereading and from deciding what to underline or highlight. This decision takes a certain amount of "deep processing."

Have you ever seen a college textbook that was inundated with yellow highlighting? McAndrew (1983) recommended that students could benefit from preunderlined text and they should be warned not to underline too much and only to underline the general ideas in the text. Harris and Sipay (1985) suggested that students should be told not to underline until they have finished reading a headed section, because waiting may reveal a summary statement. Harris and Sipay (1990) also suggested at least a two-tiered system of underlining or highlighting to differentiate between important ideas. Devine (1987) stated that "underlining is only one step from passivity" (p. 168). He suggested that making marginal comments and using personal coding systems facilitate the remembering of important points better than just underlining.

Learning to highlight or underline important ideas and facts when reading helps students learn to recognize main ideas and supporting details. Highlighting seems to help students remember important information and shorten the time needed to study for content tests. Elementary-age children especially like using highlighters. If highlighters cannot be obtained for each child, however, then the students should be taught to underline.

SQ3R

One way to activate prior knowledge and establish reader expectations about the content and the meaning of the text is to survey material before reading. SQ3R (Survey, Question, Read, Recite, Review) (Robinson, 1970) has been a popular survey technique for many years. This technique incorporates self-questioning and self-monitoring activities.

With this method, a student is taught first to *survey* a passage by looking through the material, noting titles, subtitles, key words, pictures, graphs, and summaries. Next, the student makes up *questions* that he or she expects to find the answer to by reading the chapter. Both of these techniques are designed to involve the student in what he or she is about to read. The last three steps in SQ3R are not prereading activities but involve the actual *reading,* then stopping to *recite* (or taking notes) while reading, and, finally, *reviewing* what was read.

Any study technique, including SQ3R, can be effective when it helps students focus attention on understanding important ideas in a text (Anderson & Armbruster, 1984), establish a purpose for reading, get a feel for the text through an initial survey, and read to confirm or disprove predictions (Duffy & Roehler, 1986). Many students have found that survey techniques help them anticipate what they will study. Study is therefore made more meaningful because new information is connected to what is known (or anticipated).

SUMMARY

Students understand what they read or what they hear only if they read or listen actively. Active readers have control over their comprehension (metacognition) and engage in self-questioning and predicting activities. Strategies such as self-questioning, highlighting, INSERT, and SQ3R promote more active readers.

SUGGESTED CLASSROOM ACTIVITIES

══ GOAL ══

1. *Develop active reading through:*
   a. *Self-questioning*
   b. *INSERT*
   c. *Highlighting*
   d. *SQ3R*

Week 4

1. Have students try to fill out the *Study Skills Review 2* (Student Activity 25) on their own but permit them to use their Study Skills Notebooks to find the correct answers. Review as a class and file the handout in the notebooks.

   Answer Key for Student Activity 25:

   1. Tells a story

   2. Explains facts

   3. Slow, average, fast

   4. Slow

   5. Fast

   6. Average

   7. (Answers will vary)

   8. ▽ △ ◇ ☐ ☒   (Any order is acceptable.)

   9. Get your interest, give the main idea, give facts

   10. (Answers will vary)

2. Look over the *Study Skills Checklist* (Student Activity 2) at the front of the Study Skills Notebook. Discuss the progress the students are making in study skills.

3. Explain to the students that for the next two weeks, as a class, they will be working on techniques that will help them be more active readers. Explain that one way to increase their understanding of what they read is to think about what they are reading by asking themselves questions before, during, and after reading. Assign a section of one of their narrative books and a chapter in an expository book to be read silently. Pass out Student Activity 26, *Self-Questioning—Narrative Text,* and Stu-

dent Activity 27, *Self-Questioning—Expository Text,* for them to use before, during, and after reading. (Student Activity 26 is for a narrative passage and Student Activity 27 is for an expository passage.) File these handouts in the Study Skills Notebooks.

4. Explain to your students that one very important way to become a more active reader is to think about a passage before they read it by using a KWL Chart. This is a fun way for students to activate prior knowledge and develop metacognition. Divide students into groups. Pass out the *KWL Chart* (Student Activity 28), one to each group. Introduce the subject of the brown recluse spider. Have the students write the name of the subject on the top of the paper. Then, in groups, have the students fill out the KWL Chart, listing things they are sure they know about the spider and the things they think they know or want to know. Have each group appoint a secretary to fill out the chart. After 10 to 15 minutes, have the groups share their charts. Now have students read the article on the brown recluse spider and fill in the "Learned" column of the KWL Chart.

5. Pass out another copy of Handout 28, *KWL Chart.* Again, in the original groups, have students read another passage from a textbook and compare what they thought they knew or would learn with what they actually learned. Complete this activity several times throughout the year with different materials to help students become active readers.

6. As a class, read a content area passage, paragraph by paragraph. Have students make up test questions for each paragraph as a class. Write these questions on the board as they are made. Model the process of making up good questions. After test questions have been made for each paragraph, type or rewrite the student-made questions and hand out the next day for students to take as a quiz. Repeat this activity throughout the year with different materials to help students become active readers.

7. Pass out Student Activity 29, *Writing Test Questions.* Independently have students make up a test question after each paragraph. When completed, have students exchange papers and answer each other's questions.

8. This same technique can be carried out through the process of paired reciprocal/teaching. Divide the class into pairs. Have one student read a paragraph out loud and then ask the listener two teacher-like questions. The listener answers the questions and then becomes the teacher, reading the next paragraph and asking two teacher-like questions. Switch back and forth until the passage is complete.

9. Explain to your students that another way to become a more active reader is to use the INSERT method. Give students Student Activity 30, *Insert Method,* and have students complete it independently. When everyone is finished, share readings as a group. Use this technique again with other passages from their books by placing a card along the margin or by using text material that has been duplicated.

10. Pass out a highlighter to each student in the class (use pencils for underlining if highlighters are not available.) Pass out Student Activity 31, *Highlighting,* for the students to practice highlighting the main points. Follow these suggestions:

    a. Have students read the title and discuss what students think the passage will be about. Brainstorm ideas.

    b. Read the first paragraph together and underline or highlight the key concepts. Note the main idea. It is helpful if you (the teacher) can make an overhead of the passage so the students can watch you underline the key points. Discuss why some ideas are more important than others.

    c. Do the next paragraph just like you did the first paragraph.

    d. Let the students do the next paragraph on their own and then review together.

    e. After the students have had enough practice, let the students read and highlight the rest of the passage on their own.

    f. When students are finished, go over the paragraphs that were done independently. Discuss why some ideas were highlighted and others were not.

    g. Once all the important ideas are highlighted on the page, go back over the page as a group and number the main ideas.

    h. Organize the information, highlighted into a summary.

    i. Repeat this activity periodically throughout the year.

11. Use self-questioning, INSERT, and highlighting periodically throughout the year to help your students continue to be active readers.

Week 5

1. Explain that this week you and the class will be discussing how to read an expository text. Have a chart up in the classroom that explains the following steps:

    *S*urvey: to get involved, to learn new words

    *Q*uestion: to make up questions, to get further involved

    *R*ead part of a selection

    *R*ecite: to think about the selection, to takes notes, to recite softly

    *R*eview the whole reading

2. Use a passage out of one of the classroom textbooks with boldface type, summary, pictures, and subtitles. Also, use Student Activity 32, *SQ3R Guide,* as the class works through the passage.

Survey the text to develop interest, build background knowledge, and look for new words.

Make up *questions* to develop interest and build background information.

Read a section and stop to recite.

Recite: Think about the section, take notes, or just say important facts softly. Continue to read and recite until the passage is finished.

Review: Think about the whole selection. Add to your notes.

3. Have the students complete *Matching SQ3R with Purpose* (Student Activity 33). Review the steps of SQ3R together using another passage from a classroom text.

   Answer Key for Student Activity 33:

   1. B

   2. D

   3. C

   4. E

   5. A

4. Practice SQ3R together for a week using copies of Student Activity 32.

5. At the end of the week, see how many students can remember and write down the steps of SQ3R. File all Student Activities in the Study Skills Notebooks as you progress through the activities.

Name _____   Date _____

STUDENT ACTIVITY 25

STUDY SKILLS REVIEW 2

Use your Study Skills Notebook if necessary to complete this review.

1. A narrative text is one that _____

   _____

2. An expository text is one that _____

   _____ .

3. The three reading rates are:

   _____

   _____

   _____

4. I should read a social studies textbook at a _____ rate.

5. I should read a dictionary at a _____ rate.

6. A novel such as *Tales of a Fourth Grade Nothing* should be read at a

   _____ rate.

7. Four book parts found in my science book are:

   _____   _____

   _____   _____

8. Paragraphs have five basic structures. Draw them below.

_____   _____

_____   _____

_____

9. Paragraphs are written with a purpose. The three purposes of a paragraphs are:

a. _____

b. _____

c. _____

10. List at least three things you do to help you become a better student.

I am trying to be a good student because I _____

_____

_____ .

Name _____ Date _____

STUDENT ACTIVITY 26

SELF-QUESTIONING—NARRATIVE TEXT

Fill out this sheet as you read from a narrative text. This will help you remember and understand what you are reading.

I. Before Reading

1. What is the topic? _____

_____

2. What will happen in the story? _____

_____

_____

3. What type of task will I have to complete (such as a test, a report)?

_____

_____

II. During Reading

1. Do I understand what I am reading?   YES   NO

2. In this narrative text, what is/are the:

a. Characters (list)_____

_____

_____

b. Setting (where the story takes place)_____

_____

c. Events (what is happening) _____

_____

3. State the problem or situation _____

_____

_____

III. **After Reading**

1. Do I understand what I just read?   YES   NO

2. What happened? _____

_____

_____

_____

_____

_____

_____

_____

_____

Name _____ Date _____

STUDENT ACTIVITY 27

SELF-QUESTIONING—EXPOSITORY TEXT

Fill this sheet out as you read an expository section. This will help you remember what the passage is about.

I. **Before Reading**

1. What is the topic? _____

   _____

2. What will I learn? _____

   _____

   _____

3. What type of task will I have to complete (such as a test, a report)?

   _____

   _____

II. **During Reading**

1. Do I understand what I am reading?   YES   NO

2. Do I know the main points and important details?   YES   NO

   List Main Idea:_____

   Details: _____

   _____

Main Idea:_____

Details: _____

_____

Main Idea:_____

Details: _____

_____

III. **After Reading**

1. Do I understand what I just read?   YES   NO

2. What did I learn? (summarize)

_____

_____

_____

_____

_____

_____

_____

_____

_____

_____

_____

_____

Name _____   Date _____

STUDENT ACTIVITY 28

KWL CHART

For (topic):_____

Know (What I know I know)	Want to Know (What I think I know)	Learned (What I learned)

The subject you are going to learn about is the Brown Recluse Spider. First, fill out the KWL Chart with things you know about and things you want to know. As you read, fill in the "Learned" column.

BROWN RECLUSE SPIDER

Next to snakes, spiders are probably the creepiest animals you know. But spiders are among the most useful of all living things. They live almost entirely on insects, many of which compete with people for food. By eating insects, spiders help add to the amount of food that is available for us to eat.

However, there are a few dangerous spiders, such as the black widow. Another dangerous spider is the brown recluse. It is not as famous as the black widow but it is well known to people living in Missouri.

A recluse is someone who hides from other people. This spider earns that name. It likes to live in houses, hiding under cushions and inside clothing. Because it is so shy, people often don't know that they are sharing their homes with it.

Normally, it won't bother them. But it will bite if it feels threatened or if someone puts on a piece of clothing in which it is hiding.

If that happens, watch out! While the bite is very rarely fatal, it hurts much more than a bee sting. Not only that, but the spider's poison kills skin and blood cells as well. The result is an open sore that takes a long time to heal and never completely fills in.

Fortunately, most people never meet a brown recluse spider. Still, this spider's dangerous bite and reclusive habits mean that you should stay away from it. It is easy to recognize because it has long thin legs and a black design, resembling a violin, on its back.

Like most other spiders, brown recluses are of some use to us. They help to control cockroaches. When they catch one, they inject chemicals into the unfortunate roach, wait a few minutes to let the insides turn to liquid, and then slurp down their supper. Only an empty shell is left behind.

Passage from *Amazing Animal Stories 5*, Copyright © 1981 Turman Publishing Co. Used with permission of Turman Publishing Co., Seattle.

Name _____   Date _____

STUDENT ACTIVITY 29

WRITING TEST QUESTIONS

Read the following passage and write test questions on another piece of paper.

BLUE WHALE

What animal is bigger than an elephant, bigger even that the biggest dinosaur? It's the blue whale. Blue whales are the biggest animal that ever lived. They grow to be over 100 feet long. That's one-third the length of a football field. And they weigh as much as 30 elephants.

A baby whale is bigger than an elephant when it is born! It takes a long time for a baby to get as big as its mother. But they have a long time to grow. Blue whales may live to be 80 years old or more.

Blue whales are not only big. They are strong too. One time, some hunters thought they had caught a blue whale. Really, you might say the whale had caught them. He pulled their 90-foot boat along behind him all day. And all the while, the boat's engines were going at full force in the opposite direction.

It's sad to say, but the blue whale has been hunted way too much. There may be only about 1,000 of these mighty animals left.

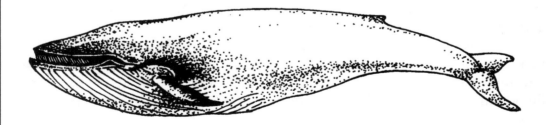

Passage and drawing are from *Amazing Animal Stories 3*. Copyright © 1980 Turman Publishing Co. Used with permission of Turman Publishing Co., Seattle.

Name _____ Date _____

STUDENT ACTIVITY 30

INSERT METHOD

As you read the following passage, place the marks below along the margin to indicate how you feel about what you are reading. This activity will help you become a more active reader.

✓   I understand
○   New information
❑   Confusing
▼   Important information

THE WOOLY MAMMOTH

How would you like to eat a piece of meat more than 10,000 years old? "Yuk!" you probably say at the thought. But that is not what a scientist said when he tried a piece of meat from a wooly mammoth that had been frozen in a glacier in Siberia for over 10,000 years. His reaction was "Yum!" That must have been what cavemen who lived thousands of years ago, during the last Ice Age, said. They, too, ate the meat of the woolly mammoth.

The wooly mammoth discovered in the glacier probably fell into a crack in the ice and died. It was preserved in almost perfect condition, so scientists found out a great deal about this ancient beast. It was almost as big as an elephant, and it had a great trunk and big, curved tusks. Its fur was long to protect it from the bitter cold.

Big as it was, the wooly mammoth was very gentle. It did not chase other animals and eat them. It was a vegetarian and ate only plants. The mammoth discovered in Siberia died before it had time to digest its dinner, so we have a good idea of the animal's diet. Its stomach contained 30 pounds of flowers, pine needles, pine cones, and moss.

Woolly mammoths liked each other's company, and they traveled together looking for food. The cavemen followed them, setting traps for the huge animals by lighting fires to scare them and then driving them off cliffs.

(continued)

Not only did our ancestors eat the mammoth's meat. They even ate its brain! They used the bones for tent frames and fuel. The oil from inside the bones acted like fire starter. They made tusks into musical instruments. They also made tiny carvings of animals from the bones and tusks. One mammoth could meet the needs of many families of cavemen for a long time.

Thanks to the long-dead caveman, we will never forget these gentle, useful beasts. Our ancestors painted many pictures of the mammoths on the walls of caves. It is a good thing they did, because there haven't been any live woolly mammoths for more than 10,000 years. No one knows why the great creatures disappeared. Perhaps they died when the weather got warmer, or maybe the caveman killed them all.

Passage and drawing are from *Amazing Animal Stories 4*. Copyright © 1981 Turman Publishing Co. Used with permission of Turman Publishing Co., Seattle.

Name _____   Date _____

STUDENT ACTIVITY **31**

HIGHLIGHTING

Read the following passage and highlight the important ideas.

DON'T PANIC

You can't tell if sand is "quick" just by looking at it. It may look dry and solid. But if you are in a place where quicksand might exist, it is a good idea to take a long pole with you to probe the ground for safe footing.

You might never get near quicksand. But even if you are careful, there could come a time when you find yourself sinking in a bed of moving sand. In this case, here are some rules which will help you escape.

Do not panic! This is the most important rule of all. Keep your head and think. You may not know that you are caught until the sand has reached your knees. Do not struggle. It will only make you go deeper into the sand.

If you have friends with you, warn them away from the quicksand. Carefully take off any load you have with you, such as a knapsack or fishing gear. Try to throw them out of the quicksand area.

Next, fall backward as gently as you can with your arms held out. Pretend you are floating on your back in water. Then as you float, begin to free your legs slowly, one at a time.

Gently squirm, roll or swim your way to the nearest firm ground. Stay relaxed and stop to rest often.

If you do have friends with you, ask them to find a support to help you. Perhaps they can use some dead tree limbs, fenceposts, rope or wire to pull you to safety.

Learn the danger signs that tell you where quicksand bogs may be found. Learn the rules for freeing yourself in case you get trapped. Tell other boys and girls about quicksand so that they too can free themselves from a quicksand trap.

The passage is from "Don't Panic" in *Essential Skills: Book 1* by Walter Pauk. Copyright © 1982 by Jamestown Publishers, Providence, Rhode Island. Reprinted with permission.

Name _____   Date _____

STUDENT ACTIVITY 32

SQ3R GUIDE

Use this checklist to help you practice the steps of SQ3R while reading one of your textbooks. Place a check by each number as you complete each step while reading.

_____ 1. **Survey**. Look over the material to be read. Read the title and subtitles. Look at the pictures. Look for new words. Put a check beside the number 1 when you have looked at the pages.

_____ 2. **Question**. Make up questions. Write them here.

_____

_____

_____

_____

_____ 3. **Read**. Place a check by the number when you have read the material.

_____ 4. **Recite**. After each section say or write what you have learned. Take notes on another sheet of paper.

_____ 5. **Review**. After reading all sections, think about what you have learned. On another sheet of paper, write a summary of the information contained in the chapter.

Name _____ Date _____

STUDENT ACTIVITY 33

MATCHING SQ3R WITH PURPOSE

The steps of SQ3R are written in order. The reasons for each step are not written in order. Match the step with the reason by drawing a line from the step to the reason. The first one is done for you.

SQ3R Steps

1. Survey

2. Question

3. Read

4. Recite

5. Review

Reason

A. Review the entire section to help yourself learn how ideas are related.

B. Look over material before reading to understand what it will be about.

C. Read the material.

D. Turn titles into questions to help you get interested in the reading.

E. Stop after each section and take notes or recite what you just learned.

Chapter
6
Promoting Active Listening

Overview

All people need to be able to listen effectively, especially in school. A strong relationship exists between listening and reading comprehension, especially as one matures. The direct teaching of listening comprehension can transfer to reading comprehension as well as enhance listening ability. Strategies such as TQLR can facilitate active listening.

Ms. Drake made sure that she had each student's attention before she began her short explanation of how to play warball. She knew from experience that her students would still have questions even after she had finished explaining the game. All of the students looked like they were listening, but were they? If Ms. Drake could crawl into the cranium of five of her students, here is what she might find.

Elizabeth does not like the way Ms. Drake dresses. She spends time during class wondering why she wears those loud colors all the time.

Rassoola sits up straight and has an interested look on his face. He has found that the teacher usually likes this posture. His mind, however, is really on what position he will play in the game.

Taylor really concentrates on the talk. He even takes notes. He especially listens for important facts. At the end of class, however, he rarely summarizes his notes by looking for main ideas and often forgets what his teacher said.

Carolyn has never done well in school. In fact, she hates school. She has good intentions of paying attention at the beginning of each day. When the teacher starts talking about things she does not understand, however, she gives up and starts daydreaming.

Bob stayed up too late last night watching a television show. He started out listening to the talk but it required too much energy. He figures he'll learn how to play warball when they get in the game. So, Bob thinks of his video game instead.

Ms. Drake's five students were hearing but they were not listening. People can think much faster than they can talk. Some educators suggest that we can think as fast as 400 words a minute but talk only about 125 words per minute. This difference allows our minds to wander. In this chapter, we will present current research on listening comprehension and its relationship to reading comprehension. We will describe the components of effective teaching of listening comprehension and suggest some strategies to promote active listening.

RESEARCH IN LISTENING COMPREHENSION

Research in listening extends back more than fifty years (Devine, 1987). One of the research-based generalizations is that listening is central to all classroom learning. People, outside school environments, spend 45 percent of their time listening as compared with only 30 percent in speaking, 16 percent in reading, and 9 percent in writing. In school, the percentages for listening go even higher. For example, elementary students spend as much as 60 percent of their time listening. Teachers would probably agree that listening is primary in all learning, in that it comes before speaking, reading, and writing in the development of all communication skills (Lundsteen, 1979).

LISTENING AND READING COMPREHENSION

The correlation between reading comprehension and listening comprehension increases from the primary grades to the intermediate grades (Sticht & James, 1984). That is, emergent readers can listen to and understand a variety of material and yet not be able to read anything. As proficient readers mature, the gap between the ability to listen effectively and the ability to read effectively closes. Some learners with disabilities may lack the verbal ability and vocabulary to read or listen successfully. Others may be able to listen and learn but their reading ability has not yet caught up to their listening ability (Gillet & Temple, 1990).

Although listening is the first language system to be developed, it is not necessarily a simple skill. Listening involves (1) *receiving* (hearing), (2) *attending* (focusing, attention span, concentrating), (3) *comprehending* (understanding), and (4) *remembering* (Leverentz & Garman 1987). Once reading and listening comprehension occur at approximately the same level, it appears that these two language processes are controlled by a very similar cognitive process. Most educators believe that training in listening comprehension will transfer and enhance reading comprehension. Boodt (1984) found that a critical-listening program improved the ability of readers with disabilities to read critically. Sticht and James (1984) found that almost all of the studies they reviewed reported a successful transfer from listening to reading.

TEACHING LISTENING COMPREHENSION

Listening activities generally begin during the preschool years with reading stories aloud. Listening skills can be taught; that is, they will improve markedly with instruction (Devine, 1982; Duker, 1968; Lundsteen, 1979). Surveys of actual classroom practice, however, indicate that little time is devoted to listening instruction.

Pearson and Fielding (1984) reached the following conclusions about teaching listening comprehension:

1. Listening training in the same skills typically taught in reading comprehension curricula tends to improve listening comprehension.

2. Listening comprehension is enhance by various kinds of active verbal responses on the part of students during and after listening.

3. Listening to literature tends to improve listening comprehension.

4. Certain types of instruction primarily directed toward other areas of the language arts, such as writing or reading comprehension, may improve listening comprehension.

5. The direct teaching of listening strategies appears to help children become more conscious of their listening habits than do more incidental approaches.

So, it seems that the direct teaching of listening comprehension is helpful to students, and evidence suggests that this listening instruction may enhance reading comprehension as well. Harris and Sipay (1990) contended that schools should place more emphasis on developing listening abilities because reading comprehension may be enhanced. However, even if listening comprehension activities had no effect on reading ability, effective listening comprehension is important for all students.

STRATEGIES TO PROMOTE ACTIVE LISTENING

Since experience, verbal ability, and vocabulary development seem to be important factors in the development of both listening and reading comprehension, reading aloud to students of all ages is imperative. The virtues of a regular time to read aloud to students cannot be overstated; it is an essential factor in all language development.

Gillet and Temple (1990) suggested a Directed Listening Thinking Activity (DLTA) as a good alternative to straight reading aloud. DLTA is similar to a Directed Reading Thinking Activity in that students make predictions about upcoming story events or state what they know about a particular topic. DLTA is an effective way to monitor listening comprehension and foster interest in listening.

Another, more structured, listening activity is the TQLR, which has four steps:

Tuning in: Thinking of what you already know about the topic.

Question: Asking yourself questions about the topic.

Listening: Listening to the speaker's words and anticipating what will be said next.

Review: Summarizing what has been said and connecting it with what you anticipated hearing.

TQLR is a structured way of getting students to engage in the effective cognitive processes that develop language abilities. Self-questioning, predicting, clarifying, and summarizing are activities that improve reading, writing, speaking, and listening.

These strategies are methods for promoting active listening. Generally, they give some overview of the topic and provide ways of connecting what the listener knows with what is being said. Listening is not a passive activity. Just like reading and writing, listening takes active involvement to be effective.

SUMMARY

Effective listening is important to be successful in and out of school. A strong relationship exists between listening and reading comprehension and educators have long believed that instruction in listening will improve reading as well. Effective instruction in listening includes the same components of developing any language ability: self-questioning, predicting, clarifying, and summarizing.

SUGGESTED CLASSROOM ACTIVITIES

GOAL

1. *Develop active listening through:*
   a. *Understanding the difference between listening and hearing*
   b. *Setting a purpose for listening*
   c. *Listening games*
   d. *Listening for details and main ideas*
   e. *Predicting*
   f. *TQLR*

Week 6

1. Although the hierarchy of listening extends through synthesis, analysis, and evaluation, it is a good start for elementary students to understand the difference between listening and just hearing. Some activities that promote active, purposeful listening follow:

   a. Discuss the difference between hearing and listening. Use examples such as the student who has the radio on but is not listening to it because he is playing ball, and the student who is concentrating on the radio and singing along with the music.

   b. Brainstorm times when people listen and when they just hear. Make a class chart.

   c. Demonstrate how a student looks when listening to a story being read and how a student looks who is only hearing the story. Get students involved in acting out, listening, and just hearing. Have students pretend to listen to a TV show and then just hear the TV show.

   d. Pass out Student Activity 34, *Listening and Hearing.* Have students complete the handout independently and then go over their work as a class. File the handout in the Study Skills Notebooks.

   e. Point out to students when they are hearing and when they are listening during the day.

   f. Ask the class to be quiet for a few minutes and really listen to all the noises around them. Discuss the different sounds students hear. Explain that they do not usually notice those sounds because they are not listening to them.

g. Make a sound as the students have their heads down on their desk with their eyes closed. Ask students to identify the sound. Increase the difficulty of this task by making two or three different sounds. Ask the students to tell what made the sounds in the order they were made.

2. The following listening games will promote active listening:

a. *Thumbs Up/Thumbs Down*: Tell students you are going to read some sentences to them. They can vote thumbs up if the sentence is true or thumbs down if the sentence is false. Read aloud several sentences, such as:

Grapes grow in bunches.

Cows can fly.

A square has three sides.

A banana is a fruit.

b. *Which Animal?*: Put pictures of three animals on display. Tell a simple short story (or more complicated story for older students) about one of the animals. Call on students to point to the picture of the animal you were telling about.

c. *Silly Sentences:* Tell the class that you are going to say some sentences with wrong or silly words in them. They must listen very carefully and raise their hand when they hear a word that does not fit. Then the student must be able to supply the correct word. Read aloud several sentences, such as:

Cows eat peanut butter.

Children sleep in wagons.

d. *Storytelling:* Students can develop their skills of effective and critical listening when they participate in a storytelling activity. Students can also sharpen their listening and memory skills as they listen for the familiar refrain or their cues in a participatory story.

e. *Simon Says:* Children must listen carefully to follow the directions or they are eliminated from the game. Make the game increasingly difficult for older students.

f. *Line Up*: Games such as this encourage students to listen carefully for directions. Select different criteria for which students may qualify to do a certain activity, such as all students who are wearing red may line up, anyone wearing sneakers can line up, and so on.

g. *Listen and Do:* Prepare a list of tasks. Explain that you will describe the task and then call on a student to carry it out. Everyone must listen because they do not know ahead of time who will be called on. Tasks could include such things as repeat a sentence, come to the front of the room and make an animal noise, stand up and turn around three times, go to the chalkboard and write your name, and so on.

h. *Instructions:* Have a student give instructions to the class so that they can make or do something, such as paper folding (origami), dance lessons, karate lessons, knot tying, and so on. Older students can later evaluate the speaker and provide constructive feedback.

i. *Listening Everyday:* Have students brainstorm situations in everyday life when listening is important. Groups can choose from this list and act out the situation for the class.

j. *Conversations:* To provide students with practice in the art of conversation and listening to each other, role-play some conversations, such as a traveler asking for directions, a person ordering a meal from an unfamiliar restaurant, a police officer investigating a crime, a doctor talking with a patient, and so on.

k. *The End:* Students listen to the teacher read or tell an interesting story. The entire story is told except an appropriate ending. Based on what they heard in the story, two groups can offer different endings and the class can vote on which they liked best.

l. *On Trial:* Select a literary character, such as the wolf in "Little Red Riding Hood," and put that character on trial. Students can role-play the lawyers, the wolf, the witnesses, and others, and the class votes on a verdict based on what they heard during the trial.

m. *Radio Days:* Allow the class to sharpen their listening skills by listening to some of the old radio shows that are available on tape. Mysteries are especially good because you can stop the tape and make predictions before hearing the actual ending.

n. *Name Game:* This is a good game to play at the beginning of the year when everyone is trying to get to know each other. The first student says his or her name only and the game continues as each student must say all of the names before his or hers in the correct order. The last student will repeat all of the names.

o. *Metacognition:* Select a situation where good listening is important, such as listening to a speaker. Then explain or think aloud what is going on in your mind as you listen. This experience helps students to understand what goes on in the mind of a good listener and serves as an excellent model.

3. Some activities that will help students note main points are the following:

a. Have the students close their eyes as you read a short descriptive poem. Then have students "scamper" or imagine what they are listening to. *Scampering* is a term used with young children that means to visualize or imagine. After you are finished reading, have the students draw a picture of the poem. Encourage them to remember the colors of the objects mentioned in the poem. Compare pictures and note differences. Read the poem again as the students look at the pictures they made.

b. Have students scamper as you read a story to them. Halfway through the story, at a critical point, stop and have students discuss what has happened so far. Then involve students in predicting what will happen next. Have students fold a piece of paper in half and draw a picture of what happened so far on one side and what they think will happen on the other side. Finish the story and let them discuss their drawings and predictions.

Missing Words

4. Have students take out a sheet of paper and number it 1 through 3. Explain that you are going to read them a short story with words missing. They are to listen carefully and write down the missing words. Read the following story:

Alesha's Gerbil

One morning, Alesha woke up and Houdini was gone. The _____ was empty. The door was closed. How did Houdini get out? Alesha looked and looked for her gerbil. Her parents looked for Houdini, too. No gerbil.

Alesha was sad all day. She thought Houdini was gone forever. Alesha _____ she would never find her gerbil. She missed Houdini. Alesha could not sleep that night. She was thinking about Houdini. Just as she was falling asleep, she felt something on her chest. It was _____ and warm. Alesha thought she was dreaming. But, no! It was Houdini. Alesha was glad to have her gerbil back. She put him back in his cage and said, "Goodnight."

Review the correct answers as a class. Repeat this exercise throughout the year using other cloze activities. (Answers: *gerbil, thought, furry*)

Following Directions

5. Have each student take out a sheet of paper. Explain that you are going to read directions to them one time only and they are to do what the directions tell them to.

a. Write your first name in the upper left corner of your paper.

b. Print your last name in the bottom left corner of your paper.

c. Draw a circle in the upper right corner of your paper.

d. Draw a triangle in the lower left corner of your paper.

e. Draw a line from your last name to the circle.

Review as a class. Repeat similiar activities many times during the year.

Listening to a Story

6. Choose a short story to read to your students. Tell them the title. Pass out Student Activity 35, *Self-Questioning—Listening*. As you read the story, have them fill out Section II. When you are finished, have them fill out Section III. Review the answers as a class. File the handout in the Study Skills Notebooks.

Listening to an Expository Passage

7. Choose a short expository passage to read to your students. Tell them the title. Pass out Student Activity 36, *Self-Questioning with Expository Text*. Proceed in the same manner as you did above.

8. Pass out Student Activity 37, *Fill in the Blanks While Listening*. Explain that you will read a passage to the students. As you read the passage, they are to fill in the blanks on the Student Activity. Read the passage at a nice even pace, allowing time for students to write. Explain that spelling is not important right now and they cannot ask you to stop and repeat the story.

Fleas, Fleas, Fleas*

To look at a flea, you would not think such a tiny insect could be so unusual. It is not much bigger than a speck of pepper. It is peppery in its actions, too. It jumps and runs the minute its host scratches at it.

Fleas can hop a foot into the air. They can make a broad jump (forward) of two feet (about .60 meters). If we could jump as well for our size, we'd be able to leap to the top of a forty-five story building. We could jump forward the length of two football fields.

You may be surprised to learn that wild animals, too, have fleas, just like dogs and cats. There are more than a thousand kinds of fleas. There are chick fleas, bat fleas, and bear fleas. There are even fleas that live on people. Some of them can live on many kinds of hosts. Others can live on only one kind of host.

Even a muskrat, swimming in the water much of the time, has its own special flea. The fur of the muskrat is so thick that water does not get into the skin. So the flea stays warm and dry close to the muskrat's skin.

You may wonder if dog and cat fleas would bite you if they got the chance. They may take a *nip* or two. But they will get back on your pet as soon as they can. Sometimes, when an animal dies or goes away, a lot of its fleas are left behind. They stay close to the animal's nest, waiting for it to return. If you come along first, they'll jump on you. This is because they have to have blood to live.

*The passage is from "Fleas, Fleas, Fleas" in *Essential Skills: Book 1* by Walter Pauk. Copyright © 1982 by Jamestown Publishers, Providence, Rhode Island. Reprinted by permission.

When you are finished, reread the story, stopping at the correct places to review answers. Complete this type of activity with different materials many times during the year using different types of material.

Answer Key for Student Activity 37:

1. one

2. two

3. wild

4. 1,000

5. chick fleas, bat fleas, bear fleas, muskrat fleas

6. warm or dry

7. people

8. blood

Listening to Write Questions

9. Explain to your students that today they are again going to make up test questions like they did last week, but this time you will read the passage to them paragraph by paragraph. After each paragraph, they will write a question for another student to answer. Pass out Student Activity 38, *Writing Questions*. Read the following passage, giving students time to write questions. Have students exchange papers and answer the questions.

Nile Crocodile*

Next time you're at the zoo, look closely at the crocodiles. Does one have big tears in its eyes? You don't have to feel sorry for him. He's crying just to keep his eyes wet.

Crocodiles are most likely never sad about the things they do. And they do some pretty terrible things, like eating people. Each year, about 1,000 people are killed by crocodiles. One big fellow in Central Africa was said to have killed 400 people in his lifetime.

Crocodiles are big. They can grow to be as big as a Cadillac car. And they are super strong. A Nile crocodile is not afraid to take on anything—even an elephant. One time a crocodile grabbed the leg of a big elephant and tried to drag it into the river. But this time, the crocodile had met its match. The elephant dragged it off to where the other elephants were. They squashed it flat. Then they picked up the crocodile and sent it flying into the tree tops.

Review the questions. Use content area books throughout the year to review this activity.

*The passage is from *Amazing Animal Stories 3*. Copyright © 1980 Turman Publishing Co. Used with permission of Turman Publishing Co., Seattle.

TQLR

10. Post a chart with the following information:

    a. Tuning in

       What do I know about the subject?

    b. Questions

       What might I learn?

    c. Listen

       What am I learning?

    d. Review

       What did I learn?

Explain each part of TQLR.

Tuning in: This means thinking of what you already know about the subject. When you "tune in," you are trying to connect new information with what you already know.

Question: Ask yourself questions such as, "What is the speaker trying to say?"

Listening: While listening, you do two things: You listen to the speaker's words and you anticipate what will be said next. Anticipation is actively thinking. Listening is not a waiting process; it is an activity.

Review: Review is the act of going over what has been said and connecting it with what is being said now and what you anticipate learning. During the review step, the listener summarizes.

Pass out Student Activity 39, *TQLR with Coca-Cola.* Have students fill out items 1 and 2 in small groups. Share information as a class. Now read the following information about Coca-Cola. Have students write down key words and ideas with each paragraph.

Coca-Cola*

Coca-Cola, which is often called Coke, is one of the most popular drinks in the world! Coke was, however, not invented as a soft drink. In the 1880s, an Atlanta, Georgia druggist, named Dr. John Pemberton, invented Coca-Cola as a tonic. It was an all-purpose medicine, made for sale in drug stores.

At this time in America, tonics were very common. Druggists and drugstore owners made medicines in the back rooms of their stores. Tonics were sold to cure everything from headaches to cancer! Now, laws control claims about what illnesses their tonics

*The passage is from Educational Publishing Concepts, Walla Walla, WA. Reprinted by permission.

would "cure." Some probably helped sick people; others did nothing and a few were probably dangerous.

Dr. Pemberton made his Coke syrup in a huge, black pot in the back room of this store. He used fruit syrup, South American cola nuts, leaves from the coca plant, and some other ingredients. He kept the exact ingredients a secret—a secret that the Coca-Cola Company keeps today.

Dr. Pemberton sold gallon jugs of his syrup to drug stores. They mixed ice and carbonated or bubbly water with the syrup. Customers would drink it for a "pick-me-up." But Coke was not a big seller as a medicine. In 1886, Dr. Pemberton sold his business to another man from Atlanta, Asa Candler, for $1750.

Asa Candler was a smart business person. He turned Coca-Cola from a tonic for illness into a drink for refreshment. He used a big advertising effort to increase sales. Coke calendars were given away. People were given coupons to get a free Coke at their local drugstore soda fountain. Banners were hung across streets. Candler even printed Coca-Cola on the glasses used in soda fountains.

Sales of Coke soared at soda fountains. One of Candler's customers got the idea to bottle Coke. But Candler was not impressed. He sold the rights to bottle Coca-Cola to Benjamin Thomas and Joseph Whitehead. Thomas and Whitehead bottled Coke so that people could drink it at home—right out of their iceboxes. They sold the rights to other bottlers across the United States and made a fortune. The bottlers had to buy their syrup from Candler. Bottled Coke soon outsold soda fountain Cokes. Candler had sold Thomas and Whitehead the rights to bottle Coke for only one dollar!

Today, soda fountains are a thing of the past and it is hard to find Coke in a glass bottle. But the soft drink in aluminum cans and in plastic bottles is as popular as ever in America and around the world. Coca-Cola is a household word in many languages!

Review as a class the key words and ideas. Have each student write a summary.

11. Continue practicing TQLR using Student Activity 40, *TQLR Review,* and content area passages from the textbooks you are currently using.

12. Pass out Student Activity 41, *The Steps of TQLR.* Have students fill out the steps of TQLR independently. Review this sheet together and file the sheets in the Study Skills Notebooks.

13. Pass out Student Activity Sheet 42, *Listening to Answer Questions.* Explain that you are going to read a passage and the class will answer the follow-up questions. Discuss the questions before you read the passage, helping the students realize that some questions can be answered correctly without listening, but not many.

133 Days on a Raft*

Poon Lin was a steward on a British tanker. The tanker was torpedoed by a German ship. Poon Lin's ship went down with all hands except Poon Lin. A raft from the tanker came floating by. Poon Lin climbed aboard. On the raft was a square piece of canvas, a short piece of rope and a small, empty water keg.

Poon Lin said the thing that saved his life was that as a little boy in China he liked to fish and made his own line and hooks. So he took the piece of rope and made a line. For a hook, he cut a piece of wood from the raft and whittled a *toggle hook* with his pocket knife. This hook is a small piece of wood sharpened on both ends like a pencil. A groove is cut in it to fasten the line so it won't slide off. The bait is cut into long, thin strips. The toggle hook is shoved into it lengthwise. When the fish swallows the bait, a pull on the line flips the hook crosswise. The hook can't be pulled out without bringing the fish with it.

Poon Lin now had the line and the hook, but no bait. But that night, he solved the problem. With his small flashlight, he *lured* a flying fish onto the raft. At daybreak, he cut the fish into long pieces for bait. He was in luck right from the start, for he was in a school of flying fish.

Yet, he wasn't always so lucky. Sometimes he'd drift for days and never catch a fish. He learned to provide for these lean days. He cut his fish into thin slices for the sun and wind to dry. Once dried in this way, they did not spoil.

These fish also gave him water. He soon found that the backbones of the fish were hollow and full of liquid. Poon Lin would remove a backbone from a fish. Then he would snap it and pour the liquid down his throat. The eyes of the fish looked watery, so he ate them. And he was right. The eyes contain about 85 percent water. When it rained, Poon Lin spread his piece of canvas on his lap like a cup. When the canvas was full, he poured the water into the keg. He wrung the water out of his clothes, too.

In this way, Poon Lin lived 133 days before he was picked up near the coast of Brazil by a fisherman. His knowledge of survival tactics and his courage brought Poon Lin to safety.

After you have read the passage, reread it and go over the answers together. Complete this type of activity many times during the year using different materials. (Answers: 1. c, 2. a, 3. c, 4. b, 5. c, 6. d)

14. Continue the paired reciprocal/teaching learning discussed in Chapter 5. This strategy develops active reading and listening skills.

15. Use the *KWL Chart* (Student Activity 28) before class discussions as a way to introduce topics and develop listening skills.

*The passage is from "133 Days on a Raft" in *Essential Skills: Book 1* by Walter Pauk. Copyright © 1982 by Jamestown Publishers, Providence, Rhode Island. Reprinted by permission.

Name _____ Date _____

STUDENT ACTIVITY 34

LISTENING AND HEARING

To listen effectively, you must attend closely, understand, and remember.

1. Divide the following words into the categories of listening or hearing: *concentrating, looking out the window, whistling, resting, looking at the teacher, understanding, remembering.*

   Listening   *Hearing*

   _____   _____

   _____   _____

   _____   _____

   _____   _____

2. Describe the way a person looks who is listening carefully to the teacher. _____

   _____

   _____

3. Describe the way a person might look who is only hearing, not listening to, the teacher. _____

   _____

   _____

4. Put an *L* beside the activities that require listening and an *H* beside the activities that require only hearing. Remember, if you listen to something, you must attend closely, understand, and remember what was said.

   Radio ___   Directions to find a certain store ___

   Teacher ___   Your friend explaining a math problem ___

   Parent ___   Your friend discussing what to wear tomorrow ___

   TV ___

Name _____ Date _____

STUDENT ACTIVITY 35

SELF-QUESTIONING—LISTENING

Your teacher is going to read a passage to you. Fill out Section I before your teacher reads, Section II during the reading, and Section III after the reading.

I. **Before Listening**

1. What is the topic? _____

2. What will happen in this story?_____

3. What type of task will I have to complete (such as a test, a report)?

   _____

II. **During Listening**

1. Do I understand what I am listening to?   YES   NO

2. Who are the characters? (list)

   _____

   _____

4. What is happening? (events) _____

   _____

5. What is the problem or situation?_____

   _____

III. **After Listening**

1. Do I understand what I just listened to?   YES   NO

2. What happened? _____

   _____

Name _____ Date _____

STUDENT ACTIVITY 36

SELF-QUESTIONING WITH EXPOSITORY TEXT

Your teacher is going to read a passage to you. Fill out Section I before your teacher reads, Section II during the reading, and Section III after the reading.

I. Before Listening

1. What is the topic? _____

2. What will I learn?_____

3. What type of task will I have to complete (such as a test, a report)?

_____

II. During Listening

1. Do I understand what I am listening to?   YES   NO

2. Do I know the main points and important details?

List Main Ideas: _____

_____

_____

List Important Facts: _____

_____

_____

III. **After Listening**

1. Do I understand what I just listened to?   YES   NO

2. What did I learn? (summarize)_____

_____

_____

_____

_____

_____

_____

_____

_____

_____

_____

_____

_____

_____

_____

Name _____ Date _____

STUDENT ACTIVITY 37

FILL IN THE BLANKS WHILE LISTENING

Read over these sentences. As your teacher reads the passage about fleas, fill in the blanks.

1. Fleas can hop _____ foot into the air.

2. Fleas can broadjump _____ feet.

3. Dogs, cats, and _____ animals have fleas.

4. There are more than _____ types of fleas.

5. Name two types of fleas.

6. The muskrat's fur helps fleas stay _____.

7. Dog and cat fleas like animals best but they will bite _____.

8. Fleas need _____ to live.

Copyright © 1995 by Allyn and Bacon.

114   CHAPTER 6

Name _____   Date _____

WRITING QUESTIONS

Your teacher is going to read a passage to you. Listen carefully to each
paragraph. Then write a teacher-like question that would go with each
paragraph. When you are finished, have another student answer your
questions.

1. Question _____

_____

Answer _____

_____

2. Question _____

_____

Answer _____

_____

3. Question _____

_____

Answer _____

_____.

Name _____   Date _____

STUDENT ACTIVITY 39

TQLR WITH COCA-COLA

Your teacher is going to read a passage to you about Coca-Cola. Practice the steps of TQLR as you work through this passage.

1. *Tune in* (What do you already know about Coca-Cola?)

_____

_____

_____

2. *Question* (What might you learn about Coca-Cola as you listen?)

_____

_____

_____

3. *Listen* (Write key words and ideas from each paragraph.)

Paragraph 1_____

_____

_____

Paragraph 2_____

_____

_____

Paragraph 3_____

_____

_____

Paragraph 4_____

_____

_____

Paragraph 5_____

_____

_____

Paragraph 6_____

_____

_____

Paragraph 7_____

_____

_____

4. ***Review***: Place a mark by the questions you had answered (#2). Review your notes. Do they make sense? Write a summary.

_____

_____

_____

_____

(continued)

_____

_____

_____

_____

_____

_____

_____

_____

_____

_____

_____

_____

5. Draw a picture of what you remember.

Name _____ Date _____

STUDENT ACTIVITY 40

TQLR REVIEW

Use this sheet to practice the steps of TQLR as your teacher reads a passage to you.

1. *Tune in* (What do you already know?)

   _____

   _____

   _____

2. *Question* (What might you learn?)

   _____

   _____

   _____

3. *Listen* (Write down key words and ideas.)

   _____

   _____

   _____

   _____

   _____

   _____

(continued)

4. *Review* (What did you learn?)

_____

_____

_____

_____

_____

_____

_____

5. Draw a picture of what you remember.

Name _____ Date _____

STUDENT ACTIVITY 41

THE STEPS OF TQLR

You have learned four steps to be a better listener. Explain what you do during each of the steps.

1. Tune in

_____

_____

_____

_____

2. Question

_____

_____

_____

_____

3. Listen

_____

_____

_____

_____

(continued)

4. Review

_____

_____

_____

_____

5. Why is it helpful to use TQLR and when should you use it? _____

_____

_____

6. TQLR is like SQ3R. Explain how these two study systems are alike.

_____

_____

_____

_____

_____

_____

_____

_____

_____

_____

Name _____ Date _____

STUDENT ACTIVITY 42

LISTENING TO ANSWER QUESTIONS

Your teacher is going to read a passage to you. Try answering the following questions before you listen to the story. Then listen to the story and change any answers you would like.

1. What would be another good title for this passage?

    a. The Great Raft Race

    b. Sailing to Spain on a Raft

    c. How to Survive on a Raft

    d. Around the World on a Raft

2. What kind of fish did Poon Lin first catch?

    a. A flying fish

    b. A shark

    c. A minnow

    d. A tuna

3. The author suggests that Poon Lin was

    a. German

    b. British

    c. Chinese

    d. Japanese

4. "The ship went down with all hands" means that

    a. the crew repaired the ship

    b. everyone on the ship sank with it

    c. only a few people are needed to run a ship

    d. quite often a ship is overloaded

(continued)

5. As used in this article, *lured* means
    a. frightened
    b. shy
    c. attracted
    d. pulled

6. Which sentence best states the main idea of this passage?
    a. Humans must use their wits to survive.
    b. Poon Lin's ship was sunk by a German torpedo.
    c. Poon Lin used a method from his childhood to catch fish to eat.
    d. Poon Lin survived thanks to his past experience and cleverness.

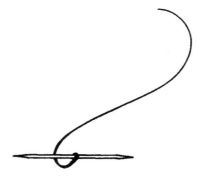

These six questions are from "133 Days on a Raft" in *Essential Skills: Book 1* by Walter Pauk. Copyright © 1982 by Jamestown Publishers, Providence, Rhode Island. Reprinted by permission.

Chapter
7
Taking Useful Notes

Overview
Learning to take good notes leads to active reading and listening. Clustering information by use of divided page, Cornell Notetaking, and charts leads to improved learning.

Benjamin had always dreaded studying for a science test. It seemed like all he did was read the same information over and over. He sat down to study his chapter on plant life and sighed when he remembered that his teacher had taught him how to use the divided page format of taking notes from his textbook. He thought he would give it a try. This particular chapter contained a lot of vocabulary words that he did not know.

He began by listing important information on the right side of his paper and key words to the left. It took him longer to take notes this way than just reading the chapter like he did in the past, but he remembered his teacher saying, "If you take good notes the first time, you won't have to go back to your book when you study for a test." That sounded good to Benjamin.

After he finished taking notes from his science book, he folded the paper lengthwise and reviewed his notes, seeing how much of the information he could remember by looking just at the key words. Much to his surprise, he remembered a lot. He planned on putting his notes away and reviewing them before the big test. Benjamin concluded that this divided note-taking system just might work.

Most educators and students realize that passive listening and reading leads to little learning. Taking notes forces students to become more active in the process of reading or listening by organizing material, "sifting through material for essential ideas, and even attempting to associate it with prior knowledge" (Harris & Sipay, 1985, p. 331). Note-taking performs a useful function in that it facilitates thoughtful reading. To take good notes, a reader or listener must select what is worth writing down by distinguishing major from minor points. It is impossible to read passively and also take good notes. Taking useful notes increases the likelihood of learning and remembering information (Smith & Tompkins, 1988).

In this chapter, organizing information through note-taking and charts will be discussed. Taking notes from lecture becomes an important skill in middle and high school; therefore, this chapter will focus primarily on taking notes from text. The research on taking notes and aspects to consider when teaching note-taking will be presented. Cornell Notetaking System and aspects of teaching students to use charts will be discussed.

RESEARCH ON NOTE-TAKING

The act of taking notes helps students learn and remember more information. Several studies conclude that students who take notes recall up to 78 percent of the information they recorded, but only 5 to 34 percent of the information is retained when students did not record the information (Kiewra, 1984). Apparently, the act of taking notes facilitates a deeper processing of the information and greater attention is focused on the information recorded.

Student-generated notes vary in volume and quality (Smith & Tompkins, 1988). Two elements, however, have been found to facilitate improved comprehension and retention of the information: knowledge of the criterion task and reviewing notes before a test. When students anticipate an essay exam, they may take notes that are more main idea and conceptual; when they anticipate an objective exam, they may take notes with more details in them. Students who take notes with the criterion task in mind are more likely to remember the appropriate information (Rickards, 1984). Teachers can help students make use of notes by constructing clear tests and telling students ahead of time what type of test will be given.

Reviewing notes before having to recall information has been found to be very beneficial to students. In fact, students who review their notes perform significantly better on achievement tests than students who do not review their notes (Hartley & Davies, 1978; Kiewra, 1985; Jacobsen, 1989). Research clearly indicates that taking notes is beneficial to the learning and remembering of information, especially when notes are reviewed before a test. In addition, knowledge of the criterion task helps students take notes that are more appropriate for the kind of recall expected of them.

TEACHING NOTE-TAKING

Discussion of note-taking is important in the elementary grades; actual practice with teacher guidance is crucial (Devine, 1987). Students need practice sessions to develop the note-taking study habit. Duffy and Roehler (1986) suggested that teachers should teach students the following:

1. To identify both the purpose of note-taking (what information is needed?) and the structure of the text (what headings, subheadings, and other devices does the author provide?)

2. To use both the purpose and the aids provided in the text to identify relevant information

3. To condense the relevant information into note form (p. 360)

Even young children should be taught that what a teacher writes on the board is usually important information. Some teachers have found skeletal notes to be helpful to students. These notes contain the main ideas that are already organized into headings and subheadings, and may provide the framework that enables students to determine the organization of the text. Teacher modeling of note-taking, such as using an overhead projector, has also been found to be helpful to students (Gall, Gall, Jacobsen, & Bullock, 1990).

Tonjes and Zintz (1981) recommended beginning with a familiar story or a textbook with good subheadings and encouraging students to make use of notes during tests and discussions. Taking useful notes is clearly beneficial to learning and remembering. The more teachers can help students take good notes with the criterion task in mind and review these notes before a test, the more success they may experience.

Some schools have found it helpful to adopt a note-taking system that can be taught and reinforced in each class. One note-taking system that is the result of decades of research and is widely used is the Cornell Notetaking Method (Pauk, 1974; 1978; 1984). In this method, the paper is divided and the important information is listed on the right side. In the left column, a few key words are written that help students remember what is written on the right side. The Cornell Notetaking System includes not only the recording of information but also reviewing of notes and reciting of noted information as well. This system has been used for years for helping students take useful notes and use them to recall information more efficiently.

USING CHARTS TO ORGANIZE INFORMATION

In their review of brain-based research, Caine and Caine (1991) suggested that teachers need to ensure that "students process in such a way as to increase the extraction of meaning" (p. 8). For some time, researchers and teachers alike have recognized that learning does not occur by memorizing isolated bits of information. Major educational movements such as thematic teaching, authentic testing, and process reading and writing attest to the readiness of educators at all levels to offer their students a curriculum that is more meaningful and connected. In fact, our earlier discussion on schema theory in Chapter 2 pointed out that students must make meaningful connections to learn or remember information.

Pearson's (1985) comment that the mind works more like a thesaurus than a dictionary supports the use of charts to organize information. Often, information in texts is provided in such a way that a chart is the most helpful way to organize the ideas. Comparisons and contrasts or simple listings of attributes may be best remembered if a chart is constructed. These charts are another form of note-taking designed to help students learn and remember better.

SUMMARY

Taking notes from text has been shown to facilitate the memory of the most important ideas if it entails processing in a way that is compatible with the task students will eventually perform (Anderson & Armbruster, 1984). Some teachers instruct their students to take good notes while first reading the text and then, when studying for the test, to refer only to the notes.

To take good notes, one must select what is worth recording and separate the major points from the minor ones and consider the relationship between ideas. Students can, and often times do, merely copy the author's words, but in order to take good notes, one must be an active reader.

The best way to start teaching note-taking skills is to begin simply. Some teachers have found it helpful to give out partial notes that require students to fill in the blanks. The divided page format has been found to be beneficial for students because it helps students highlight key concepts and important ideas. Constructing charts to organize some kinds of information has also been found to help students learn and remember information better.

SUGGESTED CLASSROOM ACTIVITIES

=== **GOAL** ===

    1. Develop note-taking skills for expository tests through:

        a. Divided page

        b. Cornell Notetaking Method

        c. Charts

        d. Index cards

        e. Use of abbreviations

Weeks 7 and 8

1. Pass out Student Activity 43, *Study Skills Review 3*. Have students fill out the activity sheet and review answers together. File the handout in the Study Skills Notebooks.

   Answer Key for Student Activity 43:

   1. Survey, Question, Read, Recite, Review

   2. (Answers will vary; however, expository books such as history, science, and the like should be listed)

   3. Study (expository book, etc.)

      Average (novel, etc.)

      Fast (dictionary, encyclopedia, etc.)

   4. (Answers will vary)

   5. (Answers will vary)

   6. (Answers will vary)

   7. Tune in, Question, Listen, Review

2. Explain that for the next two weeks, the class will work on note-taking skills. The purpose of good note-taking is to increase memory skills and shorten the time needed to study. Pass out Student Activity 44, *Unorganized Words,* to all students but do not let them see the sheet. Keep the sheet turned over until you tell them to begin. Using a timer, give the students 20 seconds to memorize the 18 words on the handout. At the end of the 20 seconds, have the students turn the page over and place it on the floor then write from memory as many of the words as they can on another sheet of paper. Share the results. Ask if any students grouped

the information to increase memory. (Examples would be animals, foods, clothes, shelters, vehicles.) Explain that the brain can remember about seven pieces of information without grouping, but when information is grouped, an unlimited amount of information can be remembered. Clustering information is the key to learning and remembering.

Pass out Student Activity 45, *Organized Words.* Again, give students 20 seconds to read and remember all 18 words on the page. Discuss the results. Most students will agree that learning is easier if information is grouped.

3. Teach the divided page format for learning vocabulary words. Have students use Student Activity 46, *Divided Page Notes,* to write down their weekly vocabulary words. Have them cover up the definitions by folding the definition section over and then test themselves. Then show them that they can fold over the vocabulary words and read the definition to test themselves.

4. Begin having your students use the divided page format for all vocabulary activities in all subjects.

5. Another version of the divided page is called the Cornell Notetaking Method. This method encourages learning by grouping information. Students list important information on the right side of a piece of paper that has been divided. Key words are written on the left. Space is left between main groups. Complete Student Activity sheets 47, *Using Cornell Notetaking System 1,* and 48, *Cornell Notetaking,* together to help students gain skills with this type of note taking. The next day, have students study Student Activity 48, then fold Student Activity 48 over so only the key words show. Let them check themselves to see how much information they can remember based on looking only at the key words.

Answer Key for Student Activity 48:

Snakes

tongue	organ of taste/smell
	it tastes the air then smells it
	forked
eyes	depends more on smell
	no eyelids
	good vision at short distance
ears	no ears—can't hear
	detects vibrations from the ground
smell	good
	track prey like a hunting dog
	nose/tongue to test odors

No important new information is in the last paragraph, so notes are not taken on that paragraph.

6. Hand out Student Activity 49, *Using Abbreviations,* and go over it together.

Answer Key for Student Activity 49:

Lincoln = pres. USA during Civil War

36" = 1 yd.

Then, together, read about the pandas discussed in Student Activity 50 and take notes using the Cornell Method.

Answer Key for Student Activity 50:

classification	not a bear relative is raccoon
characteristics	thick, wiry fur shy lives in remote parts China 4 outside of China
background	discovered 100 years ago 1936—Mrs. Harkness took 1 to USA
growing	baby = > 1/2 lb. 5 yr. = adult at 5 ft. 250–300 lbs.
food	eats a lot! bamboo = main item eats 12 hrs. a day likes tender shoots
Moscow	no bamboo eats twigs birch
sound	yodels + barks never growls
don't play with	likes to play could hurt you

7. Begin having your students take notes using the Cornell Notetaking Method in science and social studies classes.

8. Explain to your students that some information is best organized into charts to help compare and contrast information. Use Student Activity 51, *Using Charts 1,* and Student Activity 52, *Using Charts 2.*

Answer Key for Student Activity 51:

Cumulus	*Stratus*	*Cirrus*
fluffy	flat	thin
white	gray	high
high	low	feather-like
heaps of cotton	like a blanket	icy pieces
fair weather	rain	warm then rain

Answer Key for Student Activity 52:

Fish	*Amphibians*
vertebrates	vertebrates
lives in water	lives in water when young then moves to land as adult
cold blooded	cold blooded
gills	gills in water, then lungs on land
fins	better hearts—more energy

9. Throughout the year, decide as a class if material is best suited to the divided page method, the Cornell Method, or charting in some fashion. Practice these organized ways of grouping information to increase learning.

10. Material that can be organized using the Cornell Method can be put into a traditional type of outline. You may choose to practice outlining using content area material.

11. Note cards can also be used as a variation of divided page or the Cornell Method. Key words are written on one side of the card and definitions, concepts, or facts are on the reverse side.

Name _____ Date _____

STUDENT ACTIVITY 43

STUDY SKILLS REVIEW 3

Use your Study Skills Notebook if necessary to complete this review.

1. SQ3R stands for

_____

_____

_____

_____

2. List three books that you would use SQ3R to help you read and understand.

_____

_____

_____

3. List the three reading rates and a book that you would read at that rate.

Rate   *Book*

_____   _____

_____   _____

_____   _____

4. How do you like to learn spelling words? (Underline your answer.)

   a. Looking at them (visual)

   b. Spelling them out loud (auditory)

   c. Writing them (kinesthetic)

5. Write a short paragraph about holidays. Start with the main idea first, followed with at least three details. Include an ending summary sentence.

   _____

   _____

   _____

   _____

   _____

   _____

   _____

   _____

6. Write down two school goals for this coming week and two other goals.

   School Goals   *Other Goals*

   1. _____   1. _____

   2. _____   2. _____

7. TQLR stands for

   _____

   _____

   _____

   _____

Name _____ Date _____

STUDENT ACTIVITY 44

UNORGANIZED WORDS

Look at the words written below for 20 seconds. Then put this paper away. Write down as many words as you can remember. Then check the list.

house
cat
butter
cake
horse
tent
car
van
bread
shoe
dog
pants
truck
shirt
turtle
pie
sock
cabin

How many did you remember? _____

The brain can remember about seven pieces of unorganized information.

Did you remember more or less? _____

Name _____   Date _____

STUDENT ACTIVITY 45

ORGANIZED WORDS

The following words have been organized. Look at the list for 20 seconds. Then write down, on another sheet of paper, as many words as you can remember.

People
boy
girl
man
woman

Family
brother
sister
mother
father
aunt
uncle

Plants
flowers
grass
trees
shrubs
vines

Dessert
cake
pies
cookies

How many words did you remember? _____

Organized information is easier to remember.

Name _____ Date _____

DIVIDED PAGE NOTES

To learn vocabulary words and their definitions, write the word on one side of the paper and the definition on the other. Then fold the paper over so you can see only the vocabulary word. Can you recite the definition from memory? Check yourself.

Vocabulary Words   *Definitions*

_____   _____

_____   _____

_____   _____

_____   _____

_____   _____

_____   _____

_____   _____

_____   _____

_____   _____

_____   _____

Name _____ Date _____

USING CORNELL NOTETAKING SYSTEM 1

Read the following passage and take notes.

SNAKES

Did you know that a snake's tongue cannot sting? A snake's tongue is an organ for taste and smell. When a snake flicks out its tongue, it is tasting the air. Its forked tongue darts out and traps some air. The snake then moves the air to two pockets in its mouth. There, the air is smelled by the snake, much as we would use our noses to smell odors around us.

Snakes do not depend on their eyes as much as they do their sense of smell. Their eyes have no eyelids. Therefore, snakes seem to stare. Their eyes seem to be much better suited to seeing close objects than far ones. Most snakes have good vision at short distances.

Snakes do not have ears and cannot hear as we do. But snakes lie on the ground. Here they can detect vibrations such as an animal walking or an object striking the ground. Thus, Indian snake charmers give a false impression. If snakes cannot hear music, how can a charmer charm a snake with his flute?

The sense of smell is quite good in most snakes. It is known that some snakes can track their prey in the same way that a hunting dog would track a rabbit. Snakes may use both their nostrils and their tongues to test the odors on the ground and in the air close to the ground.

A poisonous snake may bite a rabbit but not follow it right then. In a little while, the poison has taken effect. Then the snake will follow the trail of its prey until it comes upon the dead animal. The senses of a snake may not be like that of humans. But they can do their job well.

The passage is from "The Senses of Snakes" in *Essential Skills: Book 1* by Walter Pauk. Copyright © 1982 by Jamestown Publishers, Providence, Rhode Island. Reprinted by permission.

Name _____   Date _____

STUDENT ACTIVITY 48

CORNELL NOTETAKING

Key Words   *Details*

Key Words

Details

_____

_____

Name _____ Date _____

STUDENT ACTIVITY 49

USING ABBREVIATIONS

Whenever possible, use abbreviations and symbols to make note-taking easy and quick.

1. Always write numbers as numbers, not words.

   1, not one   **1/2**, not one-half

2. Use abbreviations such as:

   lb. for pound   **ft.** for feet

   yr. for year   < for less than (2<4)

   > for greater than (4>2)   **w** for with

   + for and   **USA** for United States of America

   govt. for government   = for equals

Make up your own abbreviations.

_____

_____

_____

_____

3. Leave out unimportant words that don't affect the meaning, such as *the, this, in.* "Pandas live in remote parts of China" should be written "Pandas live remote parts China."

   Write the following information in note form:

   a. Abraham Lincoln was the president of the United States of America during the Civil War.

   _____

   b. There are thirty-six inches in a yard.

   _____

Name _____ Date _____

STUDENT ACTIVITY **50**

USING CORNELL NOTETAKING SYSTEM 2

Read the following information and take notes on another sheet of paper using the Cornell Method. (Divide the paper.)

PANDAS

The soft, cuddly, black and white stuffed toy with two black eyes, a black nose, and two black ears has the wrong name. It should be called a giant panda, not a panda bear, because the animal it represents is not a bear. The giant panda's closest relative is a raccoon! And the animal isn't soft, either. Its thick fur is too wiry to be used for fur coats!

Are you confused about the giant panda? Don't worry, you have lots of company. People know very little about this appealing, shy animal who lives in a remote part of China. Even today, there are only four pandas living outside China. Two are in the Washington, D.C., zoo, one is in the London zoo, and one is in Moscow in Russia.

The giant panda was discovered over 100 years ago, but it took an adventuresome woman named Mrs. Harkness to bring a baby panda out of China in 1936. Mrs. Harkness fed the panda from a baby bottle and held it in her arms for much of the trip home to a zoo in the United States.

A newborn panda is amazingly small. It weighs less than half a pound! But in five years, it grows to its adult size of five feet and weighs 250–300 pounds.

The panda has to eat a lot of food to grow so big. And what food! Bamboo is the most important item in the panda's diet. The animal's heavy jaws and powerful teeth grind on the thick, woody pieces of bamboo. The panda has to eat for twelve hours each day to get enough nourishment! No wonder the panda especially likes tender, young shoots of bamboo; it doesn't have to work so hard on them.

In Moscow, there is no bamboo. The panda there eats twigs from birch trees and seems perfectly happy. The giant panda lets people know how it feels by making a yodeling sound. Sometimes it barks. But it never growls the way bears do, and it is not a nasty animal. The giant

(continued)

panda likes to play, but it forgets how big and strong it is. It could hurt you. So if you're in a mood to play with a giant panda, play with a stuffed panda, not a real one.

Name _____ Date _____

STUDENT ACTIVITY 51

USING CHARTS 1

Read the following and fill in a chart with the information. Remember that organized information is easier to remember.

CLOUDS

Clouds are classified into three main types. Each one looks different. Knowing the types of clouds can help us predict the weather.

Cumulus clouds are fluffy, white clouds that look like heaps of cotton. They are high in the sky. Cumulus clouds are fair-weather clouds.

Stratus clouds are flat, gray clouds. These clouds are low and seem to cover the sky like a blanket. Stratus clouds are a sign of rainy weather.

Cirrus clouds are thin clouds found high in the sky. These clouds look like feathers or curls. Cirrus clouds may have tiny pieces of ice in them. These clouds often mean warm weather followed by rain.

Cumulus	*Stratus*	*Cirrus*

Name _____   Date _____

STUDENT ACTIVITY 52

USING CHARTS 2

Read the following information and make a chart.

FISH AND AMPHIBIANS

Fish are vertebrates that live in the water all their lives. Fish are cold blooded. This means their body temperature stays the same as the water around them. Fish use gills to breathe and fins to help them move.

Amphibians are also vertebrates. These animals start their life in the water using gills to breathe. As adults, they live on land and use lungs to breathe. Since amphibians live on land, they have a better working heart than fish to create more energy. Land-living animals need more energy to move on land. Amphibians, like fish, maintain a body temperature the same as their environment.

Fish   *Amphibians*

Chapter

8

Making and Using Maps

Overview

Mapping is a research-based and classroom-tested strategy that facilitates active learning by activating schema and making text structure clear.

Maria did not understand the story she was reading. The main character, Jefferson, was confusing and Maria couldn't follow what he was up to. Maria decided to stop reading for a short time and make a story map to help her follow the events of the story better. Then she did a quick character map of Jefferson. When she finished the story map and character map, Jefferson and his antics became more clear to her. Besides, now she had notes for questions she was going to have to answer on the story. Taking a break from reading was worth the time.

Story maps and chapter maps are like road maps because they show readers where they are going and where they have been when they are finished reading. Graphic representations come in a variety of forms and have been found to be helpful to students for organizing information. Some of these graphic representations are designed to show ideas in a hierarchical fashion (graphic organizers, structured overviews, and pyramids). Others show the relationships and relative importance between concepts, words, or ideas (networks, concept maps, word maps). All of these graphic representations help students put information into a manageable format, show relationships between ideas, and increase the involvement of the reader.

Although each of these graphic representations serve a useful purpose in helping students organize and learn information, this chapter will present only mapping. Research on mapping and teaching mapping for narrative and expository text will be discussed.

THEORETICAL BASIS OF MAPPING

Mapping (also called semantic maps or webbing) has been used to help students to become active readers by "triggering the brain to retrieve what is known about a topic and use this information in reading" (Crawley & Mountain, 1988, p. 3). All maps involve the development of a graphic arrangement of ideas. Major ideas are connected to supporting ideas and details by using a systematic arrangement of lines, geometric shapes, and arrows.

Mapping facilitates comprehension of text by capitalizing on the categorical nature of memory. Words or concepts in maps trigger the brain to retrieve information being stored in memory. "When this knowledge is activated and applied to text, a link is made between past experiences and text concepts" (Heimlich & Pittelman, 1986, p. 46). Comprehension and retention of text can be enhanced by using maps (Armbruster, 1979; Armbruster & Anderson, 1980; Sinatra, Berg, & Dunn, 1985).

Two bodies of literature explain the positive effects of mapping: schema theory and text structure. First, "schema is the framework for how individuals view the world...and is the basis for integrating new knowledge" (Moore, Readence, & Rickelman, 1989, p. 51). Schemata also represent individual beliefs and perceptions through which new information is filtered. Connecting new information to prior knowledge is essential before this new information can be integrated into long-term memory. Maps are a powerful vehicle for facilitating a reader's prior knowledge with the new information presented in text by having students make decisions about recording information graphically.

Second, comprehension can be enhanced by identifying the framework of the text (Beck, Omanson, & McKeown, 1982; DiVesta, Schultz, & Dangle, 1973). After a extensive review of the impact of text structure instruction on expository text, Pearson and Fielding (1991) concluded the following: "In general, we have found incredibly positive support for just about any approach to text structure instruction for expository text. It appears that any sort of systematic attention to clues that reveal how authors attempt to relate ideas to one another or any sort of systematic attempt to impose structure upon a text, especially in some sort of visual rerepresentation of the relationships among key ideas, facilitates comprehension as well as both sort-term and long-term memory for the text" (p. 832).

In summary, maps help readers identify and use the text structure to record information in a graphic representation. In the process, students become more active readers and connect more of their own prior knowledge in making decisions about how to record or organize the information. Research and practice support their use with students.

TEACHING MAPPING

Story maps are designed for use with narrative text and can be constructed from basal readers or pieces of literature. These maps generally depict elements of the story and give students practice in identifying story structure. Story maps can be used as a prereading activity or can be used after reading to review and summary the story. Other types of story maps include *story frames,* which provide the framework for a story summary; *plot relationships,* charts that help students see the relationships between events in the story; and *character maps,* which help students understand a particular character better.

Chapter maps represent all of the important ideas in a chapter or section of expository text, such as in a textbook. For younger students, paragraphs can be mapped where all the main ideas and details would be recorded. The center of the chapter map usually contains the topic. The spokes contain the main ideas or subtopics and the circles contain details or facts about the subtopics. Different kinds of maps have been designed to show various types of expository text.

SUMMARY

Mapping facilitates the activation of a reader's schema and helps the reader use text structure to record information. Story maps (narrative text) generally focus on the elements of a story, such as the setting or characters. Chapter maps (expository text) help students organize information and understand relationships between ideas.

SUGGESTED CLASSROOM ACTIVITIES

GOALS

1. Develop note-taking skills for narrative text through story maps and character analysis.

2. Develop note-taking skills for expository text through chapter maps.

Week 9

1. Pass out Student Activity 53, *Study Skills Review 4*. Have students work in pairs to find answers. Review the handout together and file it in the Study Skills Notebooks.

   Answer Key for Student Activity 53:

   1. 7

   2. Divided page, Cornell, charting

   3. Charting, divided page, Cornell

   4. Tune in, question, listen, review

   5. Survey, Question, Read, Recite, Review

   6. First sentence, last sentence

   7. (Answers will vary)

2. Review the three types of note-taking methods taught last week (divided page, Cornell Method, and charting).

3. Explain that this week, the students will learn how to make story and chapter maps. Begin with story maps.

4. Pass out Student Activity 54, *Character Map*. Explain that character analysis can be done using a character map or a compare and contrast chart. To teach this concept, first have students fill out a character map of themselves using Study Activity 54. They should write their names in the box in the middle of the page and four characteristics of themselves in the first four ovals. Then, in the remaining circles, use examples to demonstrate the four characteristics. (See the example on the next page.) Have students take this personal character map home.

Sarah's Character Map

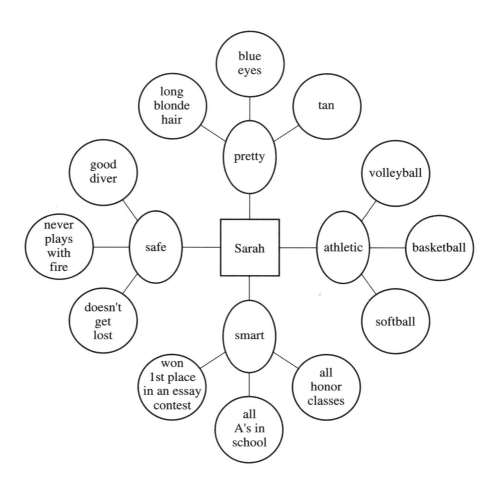

5. Pass out another copy of Student Activity 54, *Character Map,* and, as a class, map a character the class is currently studying in history or literature. File this character map in the Study Skills Notebooks.

6. Explain that another way to understand and remember character traits is by the use of a comparing/contrasting chart. Pass out Student Activity 55, *Compare/Contrast Chart.* Have each student compare and contrast himself or herself to another student, teacher, or famous person. (See the example on the next page.) Have students take this chart home.

Compare/Contrast Map

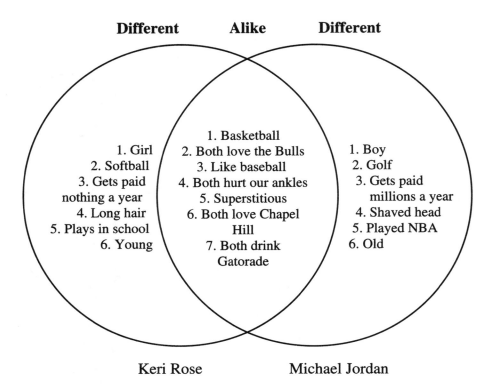

Different   **Alike**   **Different**

1. Girl
2. Softball
3. Gets paid nothing a year
4. Long hair
5. Plays in school
6. Young

1. Basketball
2. Both love the Bulls
3. Like baseball
4. Both hurt our ankles
5. Superstitious
6. Both love Chapel Hill
7. Both drink Gatorade

1. Boy
2. Golf
3. Gets paid millions a year
4. Shaved head
5. Played NBA
6. Old

Keri Rose   Michael Jordan

7. Pass out another copy of Student Activity 55, *Compare/Contrast Chart,* and, as a class, chart two characters the class is currently studying. File this chart in the Study Skills Notebooks.

8. Throughout the year, use character maps and compare/contrast charts to analyze characters in stories, novels, and history.

9. Explain to your students that they will now focus on analyzing the entire plot of a story, not just the characters. They will learn three different ways to do this: story maps, story frames, and plot relationship charts, using the story "Little Red Riding Hood." Be sure your students are familiar with this story.

a. Pass out Student Activity Sheet 56, *Story Map*. As a class, fill out the map together. File the handout in the Study Skills Notebooks.

Answer Key for Student Activity 56:

The setting/main characters:	Grandma's house Little Red Riding Hood Wolf
Statement of the problem:	Wolf wants to eat Little Red Riding Hood.
Event 1:	Little Red Riding Hood goes to Grandma's.
Event 2:	She meets the wolf in the woods.
Event 3:	She tells the wolf where she is going.
Event 4:	The wolf runs ahead to Grandma's.
Event 5:	The wolf dresses as Grandma.
Event 6:	The wolf tries to eat Little Red Riding Hood.
Event 7:	The woodsman kills the wolf.
Statement of the solution:	The wolf is dead.
Story theme (What is this story *really* about?):	Do not talk to strangers.
Values brought out in the story:	Be careful. Be safe, not sorry.

b. Pass out Student Activity 57, *Story Frame*. Fill out in pairs again using Little Red Riding Hood, and then review as a class. File the handout in the Study Skills Notebooks. You may wish to make the story frame simpler by providing space for only one character and fewer major events in the story. On the other hand, you may desire to make the outline more complicated by adding more spaces for additional characters and events. Also, you may want to vary the space provided for the various entries. You no doubt will want to tailor the story frame to fit a specific title, thereby providing a prescriptive outline, once you become more familiar with the activity.

Answer Key for Student Activity 57:

The story takes place at Grandma's house. Little Red Riding Hood is a character in the story who is taking cookies to Grandma. The wolf is another character in the story who meets Little Red Riding Hood in the woods. A problem occurs when the wolf races to Grandma's. After that, the wolf dresses up as Grandma and tries to eat Little Red Riding Hood. The problem is solved when the woodsman kills the wolf. The story ends with Little Red Riding Hood safe.

c. Pass out Student Activity 58, *Plot Relationships Chart.* Fill out as a class, again using Little Red Riding Hood, then file in the Study Skills Notebooks.

Answer Key for Student Activity 58:

Somebody: The wolf

Wanted: to eat Little Red Riding Hood

But: the woodsman killed him

So: Little Red Riding Hood was safe.

Somebody: Little Red Riding Hood

Wanted: to take cookies to Grandma

But: the wolf tried to eat her

So: the woodsman killed him.

10. Choose a literature story that the class has just read and organize the information using a story map, story frame, or plot relationship chart.

11. Throughout the year, continue to use character maps, compare/contrast charts, story maps, story frames, and plot relationship charts to help students organize narrative material.

Week 10

12. Another way to organize narrative information is in chapter summaries. When reading chapter books (novels), have students use Student Activity 59, *Story Summary.* They should write a brief summary of each chapter as they complete the chapter. Help students focus on main characters, setting, events, conflicts, and resolutions.

13. Explain to your students that they will now work on chapter maps for expository text. Pass out Student Activities 60, *Mapping Florida's Beginnings,* and 61, *Chapter Map on Florida's Beginnings.* Together, map each paragraph. The answer key is on page 155.

14. To give students practice in mapping science-related material, give students Student Activity 62, *Mapping Storms,* and 63, *Map of Storms.* Have students fill out the map on storms in pairs or small groups. Review as a class. The answer key is on page 156.

15. Continue throughout the year to take notes with content area material by using divided page, Cornell Method, charting, or mapping. Remind students that good notes increase memory and shorten study time.

Chapter Map for Florida

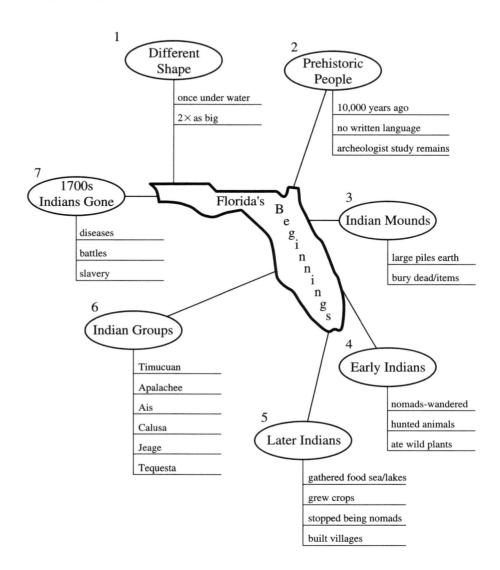

1 Different Shape
- once under water
- 2× as big

2 Prehistoric People
- 10,000 years ago
- no written language
- archeologist study remains

Florida's Beginnings

7 1700s Indians Gone
- diseases
- battles
- slavery

3 Indian Mounds
- large piles earth
- bury dead/items

6 Indian Groups
- Timucuan
- Apalachee
- Ais
- Calusa
- Jeage
- Tequesta

4 Early Indians
- nomads-wandered
- hunted animals
- ate wild plants

5 Later Indians
- gathered food sea/lakes
- grew crops
- stopped being nomads
- built villages

Chapter Map for Storms

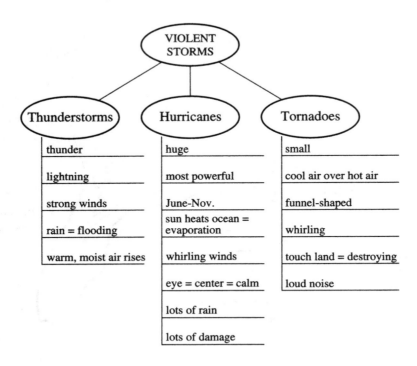

Name _____ Date _____

STUDENT ACTIVITY 53

STUDY SKILLS REVIEW 4

1. How many pieces of unorganized information can the brain typically remember? _____

2. Name three ways to organize information.

   _____

   _____

   _____

3. Which of the three note-taking systems would you use when:

   a. Comparing birds and mammals?

   _____

   b. Learning vocabulary words and definitions?

   _____

   c. Studying a chapter in social studies?

   _____

4. What does TQLR stand for?

   1. _____   2. _____

   3. _____   4. _____

(continued)

5. What does SQ3R stand for?

_____

_____

_____

_____

_____

6. When reading a paragraph, where is the main idea most likely to be found? (two choices)

_____

_____

7. Decide on two school-related goals for this week.

_____

_____

_____

_____

_____

_____

_____

_____

_____

_____

Name _____   Date _____

STUDENT ACTIVITY **54**

CHARACTER MAP

On the next page, fill out a character map of yourself.

1. Place your name in the box in the middle of the character map.

2. List four characteristics of your self that describe who you are, what you do, what you like, how you look, and so forth.

    a.

    b.

    c.

    d.

3. Now write these characteristics in the ovals attached to the box.

4. In the three circles attached to each oval, write words that demonstrate or explain your characteristics.

(continued)

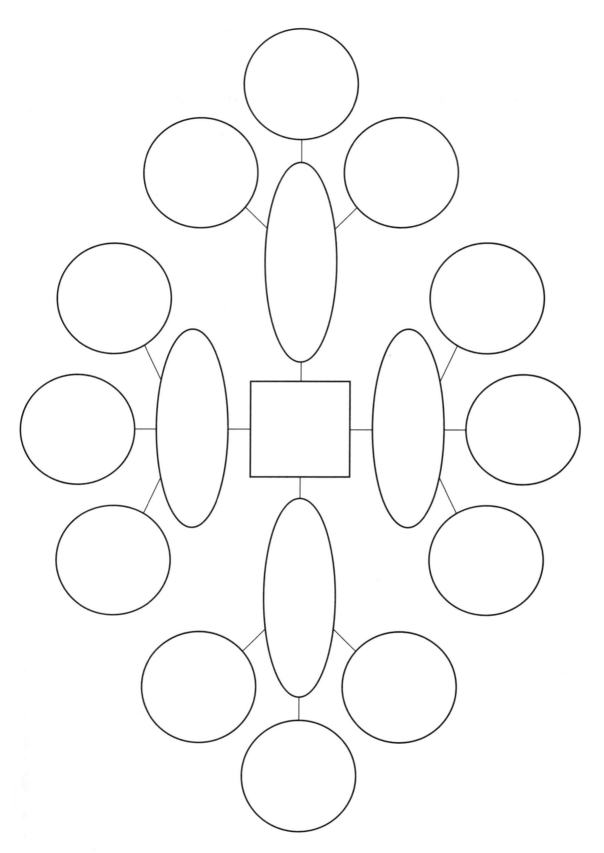

Name _____ Date _____

COMPARE/CONTRAST CHART

On the next page, compare and contrast yourself with another person.

1. Write your name under the circle to the left.
2. Write the other person's name under the circle to the right.
3. In the middle, where the circles overlap, write the things you have in common with the other person.
4. In the circle on the left, write characteristics about yourself that the other person does not share with you.
5. In the circle on the right, write characteristics about the other person that are not shared by you.

Now you can see how you and the other person are the same and different.

(continued)

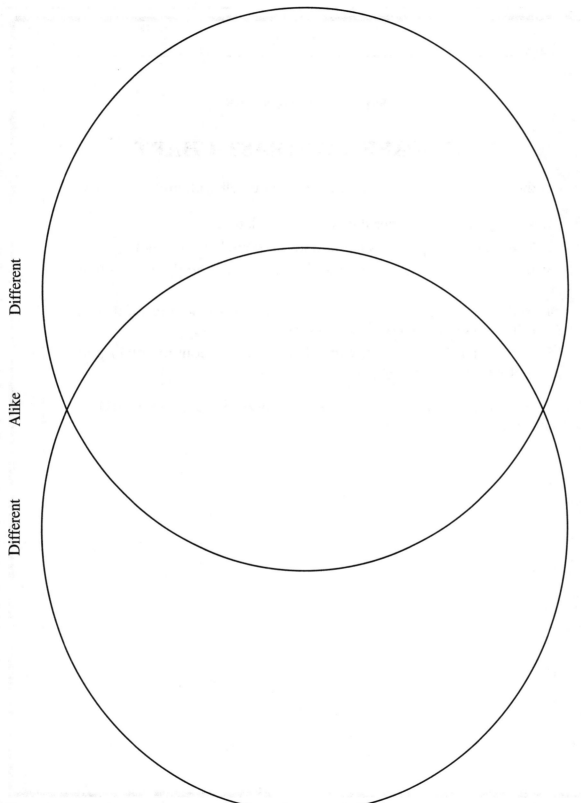

Different   Alike   Different

From James M. Macon, Diane Bewell, & MaryEllen Vogt, *Responses to Literature: Grades K–8*. Copyright © 1991 by the International Reading Association, Inc. Reprinted with permission of the International Reading Association.

Name _____ Date _____

STUDENT ACTIVITY 56

STORY MAP

On the next page, fill out a story map of "Little Red Riding Hood."

1. List the setting and two main characteracters.
2. State the problem.
3. List the events.
4. State the solution.
5. State the theme.
6. State the values that are raised in the story.

Now you can quickly and easily "see" the main characters, events, and theme on one sheet of paper. Story maps are good ways to organize information.

(continued)

The setting/main characters

Statement of the problem

Event 1

Event 2

Event 3

Event 4

Event 5

Event 6

Event 7

Statement of the solution

Story theme (What is this story *really* about?)

Values brought out in the story

From James M. Macon, Diane Bewell, & MaryEllen Vogt, *Responses to Literature: Grades K–8.* Copyright © 1991 by the International Reading Association, Inc. Reprinted with permission of the International Reading Association.

Name _____ Date _____

STUDENT ACTIVITY 57

STORY FRAME

The story takes place _____

_____ .

_____ is a character in the story who

_____ .

_____is another

character in the story who _____ .

A problem occurs when_____

_____

After that, _____

_____

and _____ .

The problem is solved when_____

_____ .

The story ends with _____

_____ .

From James M. Macon, Diane Bewell, & MaryEllen Vogt, *Responses to Literature: Grades K–8.*
Copyright © 1991 by the International Reading Association, Inc. Reprinted with permission of
the International Reading Association.

Name _____   Date _____

STUDENT ACTIVITY 58

PLOT RELATIONSHIPS CHART

Somebody	Wanted	But	So

From James M. Macon, Diane Bewell, & MaryEllen Vogt, *Responses to Literature: Grades K–8.*
Copyright © 1991 by the International Reading Association, Inc. Reprinted with permission of
the International Reading Association.

Name _____ Date _____

STORY SUMMARY

As you read your book, write a brief summary of each chapter in the boxes below. Be sure to include main characters, setting, events, problems, and solutions.

Chapter 1
Chapter 2
Chapter 3
Chapter 4
Chapter 5
Chapter 6

Name _____ Date _____

STUDENT ACTIVITY 60

MAPPING FLORIDA'S BEGINNINGS

Make a map of the following information by filling in the blank map.

FLORIDA'S BEGINNINGS

Florida did not always have the shape it has today. In fact, many geologists (scientists who study the earth) believe that Florida was once underwater. They also believe that there was once a time that the sea level dropped so low that Florida was at least twice as big as it is today.

Scientists believe that people lived in Florida about 10,000 years ago. We call these people prehistoric people because they had no written language. Since these prehistoric people did not write about their lives, it is hard for us to know how they lived. What we do to learn about their way of life is to study the objects of their lives. Such items as broken pottery, human bones, and tools help us learn about their lives. Scientists who study the remains of people from years and years ago are called archeologists.

Archeologists have discovered many Indian mounds throughout Florida. Indian mounds are large piles of earth, sometimes looking like large ant piles. These mounds are often larger than houses. Indians used these mounds to bury their dead. As more people died, the mounds grew higher and wider. The Indians often buried items that belonged to the dead. Archeologists study these burial mounds to find out more about these early Indians.

Archeologists believe that prehistoric people lived throughout Florida. They wandered across the land in search of food. They hunted wild animals and ate wild plants. These prehistoric people were called nomads. A nomad is a person who travels from place to place in search of food. A nomad does not live in one place.

As the wild animals left, or began to die off, these nomads learned to find food in other ways. They began to gather food from the sea and from the lakes. They also learned how to grow their own crops. As they learned these new ways of life it was no longer important to travel in search of food. They stopped being nomads and began to live in one place. They built permanent villages and established their own areas or territories.

By the time the early Spanish explorers came to Florida, many Indian tribes had set up villages. The six most important groups were the Timucuan, Apalachee, Ais ,Calusa, Jeaga, and Tequesta. By the 1700s, most of the Indians had died or left Florida. Many died from diseases brought over by the white men. Others died in battle. Still other Indians were taken in slavery by the white man.

Passage from *Florida Studies*, Copyright © 1984 Southwinds Press/George F. Cram. Used by permission.

Name _____   Date _____

STUDENT ACTIVITY 61

CHAPTER MAP ON FLORIDA'S BEGINNINGS

1 Different Shape

2 Prehistoric People

7 1700s Indians Gone

Florida's Beginnings

3 Indian Mounds

6 Indian Groups

5 Later Indians

4 Early Indians

Name _____ Date _____

STUDENT ACTIVITY 62

MAPPING STORMS

STORMS

Thunderstorms
Thunderstorms can be violent storms. Thunder, lightning, and strong winds can accompany a thunderstorm. Heavy rains can cause flooding. Thunderstorms occur when warm, moist air rises rapidly. Stay inside when thunderstorm come.

Hurricanes
Hurricanes are huge storms. These storms are the most powerful storms on earth. Hurricanes usually develop between June and November. The sun heats the ocean near the equator and large amounts of water evaporates. This causes a hurricane to form. These storms consist of whirling winds. A center of calm air, called an eye, is in the middle of the whirling winds. Heavy winds and lots of rain can cause damage. Hurricanes are very violent storms.

Tornadoes
Tornadoes are small but very violent storms. These storms occur when cool air moves over hot air and the hot air then rises. These funnel-shaped whirling storms travel across the earth, touching land as they move. They destroy whatever is in their path. A loud noise, which sounds like a train, is often heard before the storm strikes. If you hear this noise, move inside quickly.

Name _____ Date _____

STUDENT ACTIVITY 63

MAP OF STORMS

On the next page, map the three violent storms as you read Student Activity 62.

1. Write the name of each storm in the oval at the top of the page.
2. Read about thunderstorms and write at least 5 facts about thunderstorms under the oval.
3. Read about hurricanes and write 8 facts about hurricanes under the oval.
4. Read about tornadoes and write 6 facts about tornadoes.

Now you have a one-page, easy-to-read study sheet that lists all important facts about storms. Maps are a great way to organize information so you can remember what you have read.

(continued)

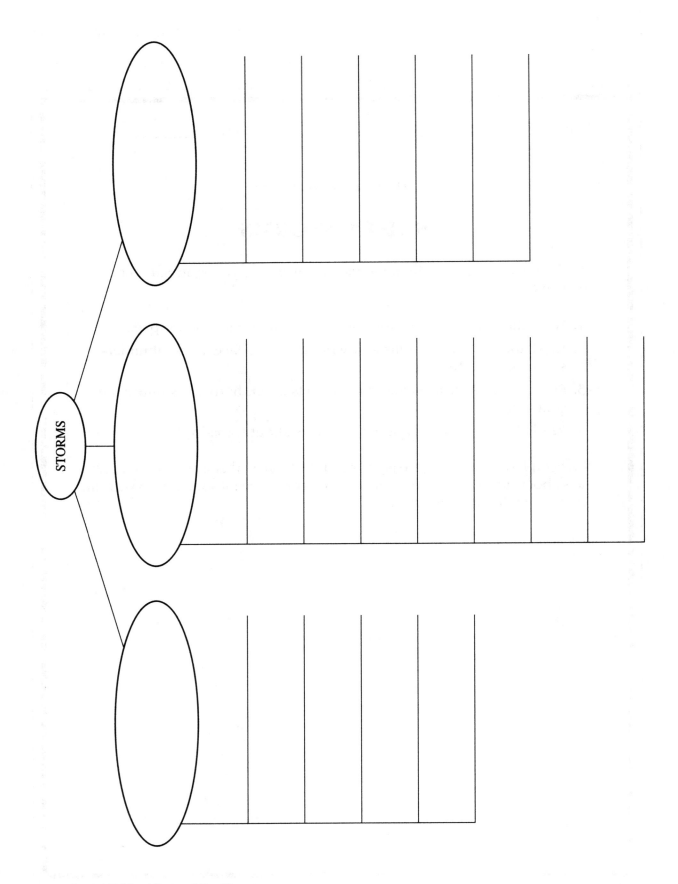

Chapter
9

Answering Essay Questions and Writing Summaries and Reports

Overview

Demonstrating knowledge involves organizing information and identifying main ideas and important details. Writing to learn activities such as answering essay questions, writing summaries, and writing reports facilitates the recall of information.

Lamar was determined to put study skills to work during the unit on mammals. Her teacher told her that study skills save time because they help organize information and remember more. Besides, Lamar's grades on the last report card did not seem to reflect the time she spent studying.

During the videos she watched and during her reading about mammals, Lamar used the divided-page method to list new vocabulary words. She then organized the chapter into a map that contained everything she knew about mammals and studied this map before the test. The test contained three essay questions. During the test, Lamar read the questions carefully, underlined the key words, and jotted down the main points before writing her paragraph. The time was well spent; she received an A on the test.

Lamar's teacher also assigned a report on a mammal. Lamar chose horses, took notes using the Cornell Method to organize the information into units, and wrote a report using a good introduction and concluding paragraph. Although it took time to organize information and identify the most important ideas for her essay questions and report, the effort seemed worth it because the actual writing seemed easy.

Demonstrating knowledge involves organizing information and identifying the main ideas. In fact, determining, organizing, and reporting the main ideas of any learning event (text, film, discussion) is what the demonstration of knowledge is all about. The process of organizing information into important and less important ideas facilitates the recall of information.

Lamar began her study of mammals with the criterion task clearly in mind. She knew that she would have to take a test, which included essay questions, and write a report on horses. All of these learning activities involve working with main ideas and details. Students who keep the criterion task in mind while organizing information are generally more successful in their studying.

In this chapter, writing to learn will be discussed. Three learning activities (answering essay questions, writing summaries, and writing reports) that involve organizing work, as well as identifying and using main ideas and important details, will be presented. The process of completing these three activities helps students learn better and demonstrates to teachers how well students they have mastered the material.

WRITING TO LEARN

Most writing assignments given to students to promote learning and measure performance are no longer than a sentence (Applebee, 1981). That is, students seem to spend more time filling in the blank, matching, and answering objective questions than writing about what they have learned. Additionally, most writing assignments require that students report back what they read rather than synthesize information, summarize it, and add their own perspective.

Reading has dominated the classroom for many years. Only recently have educators discovered the potential of writing to learn. When students have the opportunity to explore the meaning of what they read by elaborating and summarizing it, they extend their thinking (Newell & Winograd, 1989). Writing essays, summaries, and reports are activities that are generally expected in intermediate, middle, and high school classrooms. Although these learning strategies are somewhat complex, much can be done during the elementary years to prepare students to distinguish between important ideas and less important ideas and to record these main ideas succinctly. Not only does the product (essay questions, summaries, reports) become increasingly important as school years progress but these strategies develop metacognitive abilities as well.

ANSWERING ESSAY QUESTIONS

Essay questions enable students to step back from a body of information, synthesize and organize it, and report what they have learned. Thinking skills are always involved when answering essay questions. Students may be asked to compare and contrast (How is a plant cell different from an animal cell?), explain a concept (What is heat?), or describe something (Describe the water cycle). Langer (1986) found that different types of assignments and questions lead to different types of thinking. Essay questions facilitate reconceptualizing content and focusing on larger issues or topics.

Students must be able to perform two tasks to answer an essay question successfully: (1) identify the type of thinking required (compare/contrast, list, describe) and (2) recall and report the content. Beyer (1987) suggested that thinking abilities can be strengthened if, periodically, students are asked to write a narrative explaining to another student how to employ a selected thinking operation to complete a specific task. This narrative may accompany the essay question, but, of course, would not be graded.

Essay questions present a special challenge for students and require systematic instruction. Students need practice sessions using methods for writing good answers to essay questions and need lots of teacher guidance and feedback. Although essay questions are often difficult for students, they can be an effective vehicle for developing thinking skills among elementary school children.

WRITING GOOD SUMMARIES

Writing a summary is a complex activity and involves condensing information to the main ideas and reporting the gist or essence of text. Students must remember the most important ideas and omit the unimportant or irrelevant ideas. Paraphrasing and condensing information are two important skills in writing a good summary. Additionally, sensitivity to text structure is also necessary to identify the most important ideas. The activities involved in summarizing (identifying main ideas, paraphrasing, condensing information, sensitivity to text structure) are important metacognitive skills and, when internalized by the student, naturally lead to more thoughtful reading.

Summarizing information from text is a valuable study technique but is used infrequently in content areas (Vacca & Vacca, 1989). In the past decade, the effectiveness of summarizing as a learning strategy and as a study skill is well documented. Just as with answering essay questions, the process of summarizing facilitates learning and metacognitive abilities and the product is useful to recall information for a later criterion task.

Research on Summarizing

Writing summaries will force learners to use in-depth processing on the more important ideas in the text (Tei & Stewart, 1985). Composing a summary is a complex task that requires considerable skill (Baker & Brown, 1984). Research has documented clear developmental trends in summarizing (Brown & Day, 1983; Brown, Day, & Jones, 1983; Paris, Wasik, & Turner, 1991; Taylor, 1986; Winograd, 1984). That is, older and more proficient readers summarize better than younger and less skilled readers. More capable fourth- and fifth-grade summary writers planned before they wrote, used text structure as an aid in selecting and generalizing, recorded important information in their own words, and monitored the text to evaluate their own accuracy.

Effective summary writing is one of the abilities that differentiates good from poor readers, and learning to summarize can improve poor readers' comprehension (Brown & Day, 1983). Teaching students to summarize can facilitate learning by helping readers clarify the meaning and significance of text (Brown, Campione, & Day, 1981; Doctorow, Wittrock, & Marks, 1970; McNeil & Donant, 1982). Self-directed summarization can be an excellent comprehension monitoring activity (Hidi & Anderson, 1986). Poor readers, however, do not readily engage in self-directed summarization (Palincsar & Brown, 1983). So, although summary writing is a complex activity, it can be taught, and the teaching of summarizing improves comprehension and recall of information.

Teaching Summary Writing

Summary writing is difficult for students to learn, especially for children below the sixth-grade level. Students in the primary grades often have difficulty in identifying the central ideas of a text and condensing it into a concise form (Noyce & Christie, 1989). Therefore, initial attempts to teach summary writing should be as simple as possible. Hidi and Anderson (1986) suggested the following guidelines for teaching students to write good summaries.

1. Use brief passages at first and begin with the more familiar narrative text.

2. Texts should be well organized and contain vocabulary and content that is familiar to students.

3. Text should be in view when young students write summaries. This reduces the burden of remembering information and focuses on the skill of summarizing. As students become more proficient in summarizing, the text can be taken away.

4. Initial summaries should be just slightly shorter than the original text, which may involve a retelling of a story with the deletion of only the most trivial details.

5. Initial summaries should be writer based. That is, initial attempts should be more like journal entries, where the main focus is on content, not on the mechanics of writing. Once students become more proficient at writing summaries, they can be shared with other students and the teacher. Peer-editing groups are a good way to help students revise and perfect summaries prior to publication or grading (pp. 487–491).

Students should have sufficient practice in summarizing orally so they can easily and confidently summarize aloud before being asked to compose written summaries. It is important for children to see and hear the teacher model summarizing. Teachers can summarize the day's activities, a story read aloud, or events in the lunchroom. Students can be asked to summarize math and science lessons, give brief oral or written accounts of books they have read, or summarize Show and Tell. Students who are not fluent writers can use tape recorders to record their summaries (Temple & Gillet, 1989).

In summary, daily classroom activity provides numerous opportunities for teachers to model and for students to practice summarizing. Teachers must model what they want students to be able to do. Research clearly indicates that summarizing is an important metacognitive and comprehension skill that deserves systematic attention in the classroom. Granted, students can not be expected to become proficient at summarizing in the elementary grades, but much can be done to develop the ability during these years.

WRITING GOOD REPORTS

One of the most difficult tasks for elementary-age students is writing informational reports. The problem seems to be that report writing requires a more formal style of language than they are accustomed to writing (Fisher & Terry, 1990). To many students, writing a report means copying out of an encyclopedia. Like answering essay questions and writing good summaries, report writing is complex and involves components such as taking notes, organizing information, and the actual writing of the report.

Essentially, a report is a piece of writing in which students must take a body of information, interpret and summarize it, give it some personal perspective, and present it in some acceptable form (Nessel, Jones, & Dixon, 1989). Report writing has two purposes: (1) to help learners understand material better by organizing and shaping it for others and (2) to provide teachers with immediate feedback on the success of lessons (Devine, 1987). Although report writing is often a test of will and tenacity, when properly introduced, this task can serve as a vehicle for learning new information and new skills.

Teaching Report Writing

During the elementary grades, a report should not be a task only to receive a grade or to prepare for stiffer report requirements the next school year. Rather, a report should be a task to "unearth interesting information and put it in a form that would be interesting to others" (Nessel, Jones, & Dixon, 1989, p. 217). Suggestions for activities that prepare students to write good reports without the usual pain and agony including prewriting activities, recording information, and reports without words.

Good reports follow from good prewriting activities because report writing is merely an extension of the reading-thinking process (Nessel, Jones, & Dixon, 1989). Before beginning to read about the topic, students should be encouraged to brainstorm the topic using a KWL (Know, Want-to-Know, Learn) (Ogle, 1989) strategy or mapping activity. To avoid copying from encyclopedias, teachers should supply only source materials that are easy to read. "Children cannot paraphrase from an encyclopedia they cannot read and understand, they can only copy" (Temple & Gillet, 1989, p. 288). Source material should be displayed and discussed so that going to the library does not become an overwhelming and defeating exercise.

Students can learn much about report writing by collecting and recording their own data before writing. Observations, surveys, measurements, and comparisons both in and out of the classroom provide rich opportunities for students to collect and organize data and construct a written report of the results. Children can use experiences with recording as a basis for more formal report writing later in their school careers.

Devine (1987) suggested that "reporting without words" can be a useful technique to encourage students to decide what is the most important information to present, how to organize that information, and how to present it in a form that lends itself to understanding the material. Visual representations of information include pie graphs, bar graphs, organizational charts, models, maps, and pictographs. A report without words can reveal much about a student's understanding of a topic. Guiding questions can help students read and interpret information. Devine (p. 272) suggested some of the following questions: What is the title? What is its purpose? Why are you using it? What type is it? Are there verbal explanations? Where? Do you understand them? What symbols are used? What do the symbols mean? Is a key given? Visual representations of information can help students organize and synthesize information and can give the teacher insights into what students have learned.

Beach (1983) suggested that students should be taken through the report writing process at least four times a year. Teachers can assure a successful experience if students have input into selecting their own topic, sources are organized for students, prewriting activities are designed, and immediate feedback is given.

SUMMARY

The process of answering essay questions, writing summaries, and writing reports helps students organize information and identify main ideas and important details to recall at a later time. Essay questions enable students to synthesize and organize information. Writing good summaries involves condensing information to the main ideas. Report writing involves taking notes, organizing information, and the actual writing of the report. These activities help students organize and recall information—tasks that are valuable throughout a student's school career and beyond.

SUGGESTED CLASSROOM ACTIVITIES

══ GOAL ══

1. *Develop writing skills for summaries, reports, and essays through:*
   a. *Organizing ideas before writing*
   b. *Writing a good introduction, including facts, and writing a good conclusion*
   c. *Using transition words and adjectives*
   d. *Editing*
   e. *Reading the essay question carefully and underlining key words*

Week 11

Summary Writing

1. Pass out Student Activity 64, *Study Skills Checklist*. Have the students fill out the form independently, then share with each other. File the handout in the Study Skills Notebooks.

2. Explain that this week the students will work on writing good summaries. Start by making a class list of activities completed during the school day, including unimportant events. When the list is complete, mark off unimportant details to demonstrate the process of condensing material. Then, again as a class, write a brief summary using only important events from the day. Demonstrate the need for a topic or introductory sentence and a concluding sentence.

3. Involve students in oral summaries throughout the day. For example, "Tell me *briefly* what happened in Art, P.E., and Music." Demonstrate the difference between including all information and only the important information.

4. Have the students write a brief summary of what they did on a vacation. Be sure they start with a fact list and then cross off details that were not important. Be sure they use an introductory sentence and end with a concluding sentence.

5. Have each student choose a story he or she is very familiar with and write a summary of the story (for example, *Little Red Riding Hood, The Little Engine That Could, Snow White, Johnny Appleseed*, etc.). You may want to choose one as a class and together make a fact list and write a summary before asking students to write one independently. Be sure to demonstrate including only important information.

6. Pass out Student Activity 65, *Writing a Good Summary 1*, and together highlight main ideas and important facts about the dodo bird. Use this time to review paragraph purpose and paragraph shapes. Now, as a class, brainstorm several choices for introductory sentences and concluding sentences. Independently have students write a summary while looking at what they highlighted. Allow students to use one of the choices brainstormed for the topic and ending sentences, or let them think of their own. As they write, encourage condensing and paraphrasing. Possible beginning sentences might be: Dodo birds once really existed; Dodo birds were really dumb animals; Did you know there once was an animal called a dodo bird? Possible concluding sentences might be: The dodo was a very unusual animal; The dodo bird is a good example of why we must be careful not to let animals become extinct.

7. Repeat the preceding activity using Student Activity 66, *Writing a Good Summary 2*, but this time do not brainstorm beginnings and endings together. Review each student's paper to be sure the summary does contain a topic sentence, a concluding sentence, and a good condensing of facts in the middle. File this in the Study Skills Notebooks.

8. Throughout the year, have students write summaries of content passages and narrative passages. Always have students use some type of prewriting activity such as highlighting, mapping, or creating a fact list. Be sure they use a topic sentence and a concluding sentence. Teaching good writing skills will require teachers to review writing samples independently with students periodically.

Weeks 12 and 13

Report Writing

1. A good way to introduce the concept of report writing is to have students prepare a report without words. For example:

   a. Use pictures to report on their life.

   b. Demonstrate the water cycle through a drawing.

   c. Use charts to show the life cycle of a frog.

2. Explain to your students that writing a good report is very similar to writing a good summary, only a report is longer. The first step is to organize information before writing, as they did with the summaries. They also need to write a good introduction, but this time the introduction will be a whole paragraph, as will the conclusion. Each important fact will also be a paragraph instead of a sentence.

3. Pass out Student Activity 67, *Outline of Your Life*. Explain to the class that they are going to write a five-paragraph report on their life. Begin by having each person fill out the outline. The next day, pass out Student Activity 68, *Transition Words*. Go over this sheet together and have students begin working on their five-paragraph report on their life using

the outline they filled out already. Walk around the room and monitor each paragraph and the use of transition words. When students finish, pass out Student Activity 69, *Editing Checklist.* Have students edit their report. File this report along with Student Activities 67, 68, and 69 in the Study Skills Notebooks.

4. Now have students choose a famous person—anyone they would like, such as a president, an athlete, or a heroine. Have them fill out Student Activity 70, *Map of a Famous Person,* and write a four-paragraph report, finishing with an editing checklist. They will need to know more than a few details about this person to write a four-paragraph report.

5. At least four times during the school year, involve the students in more lengthy reports. Let students choose what they want to report on and then provide guidance as to what prewriting activity would be most helpful. For example, if students want to report on storm systems, encourage them to use a map to organize information before writing. Use Student Activity 71, *Editing Checklist,* and encourage descriptive and transition words.

Week 14

Answering Essay Questions

1. Explain that writing a good answer to an essay question is very similar to writing a summary or report. The big difference is to be sure to answer a specific question presented by learning how to read key words. Pass out Student Activity 72, *Essay Terms.* Review and discuss together then file in the Study Skills Notebooks.

2. Pass out Student Activity 73, *Practice with Essay Terms.* Together, have the students circle the key essay terms and underline the key words to write about.

Answer Key for Student Activity 73:

1. (List) the three parts of the human circulatory system.

2. (State) what heat is.

3. (Name) and (describe) the four violent storm systems.

4. (Explain) the three states that water can take, and the temperature for each state.

5. (Describe) four landforms found in the United States.

6. (Diagram) the water cycle.

7. (Explain) what latitude is.

8. (Explain) three ways Matt demonstrated courage in *The Sign of the Beaver.*

    9. (Compare and contrast) plant cells and animal cells.

   10. (Summarize) the events that led to the Revolutionary War.

   11. (Define) what the term photosynthesis means.

3. Pass out Student Activity 74, *How to Write a Good Answer to an Essay Question.* Go over the handout together and encourage students to learn the steps. File in the Study Skills Notebooks.

4. Pass out Student Activity 75, *Review of Essay Writing Steps.* Have students fill out the form independently and then review as a class. File in the Study Skills Notebooks.

   Answer Key for Student Activity 75:

   1. question

   2. key

   3. ideas

   4. introduction

   5. descriptive

   6. concluding

   7. question

   8. question

   9. edit

5. Pass out Student Activity 76, *Answering Good Essay Questions 1.* Have the students answer the essay question by following the steps listed.

6. Have students complete Student Activity 77, *Answering Good Essay Questions 2.* This question has two parts.

7. Throughout the year, have students answer essay questions and create their own essay questions.

Name _____   Date _____

STUDENT ACTIVITY **64**

STUDY SKILLS CHECKLIST

		YES	*NO*
1.	I want to learn.	_____	_____
2.	I keep an assignment pad.	_____	_____
3.	I find a good place to study without distractions.	_____	_____
4.	When I lose concentration, I can get myself back on track.	_____	_____
5.	I set goals.	_____	_____
6.	I look for key words and main ideas when reading.	_____	_____
7.	I listen carefully.	_____	_____
8.	I take organized notes.	_____	_____
9.	I recite information out loud.	_____	_____
10.	I take breaks when I study.	_____	_____

Name _____ Date _____

STUDENT ACTIVITY **65**

WRITING A GOOD SUMMARY 1

Read and highlight the following passage. Be careful to highlight only a few very important ideas.

THE DODO BIRD

You've heard the sayings "dumb as a dodo" and "dead as a dodo." There's a good reason why these sayings came to be. The dodo was a bird that lived on some islands near Africa. And it was really dumb. It was so fat that when it tried to run, its stomach would rub on the ground. It was bigger than a turkey, but it had only tiny little wings and couldn't fly.

About the year 1600, settlers came to the islands where the birds lived. They called them dodos from a Portuguese word meaning "stupid." The birds were killed by the settlers and their dogs. The dodos were too dumb to run away.

A stuffed dodo was put in a British museum. After awhile, it started to rot. The people at the museum were going to throw it out. But the head and one foot were still good. So the museum saved them. And that's all that is left today of the dodo bird.

Passage and drawing are from *Amazing Animal Stories 3*. Copyright © 1980 Turman Publishing Co. Used with permission of Turman Publishing Co., Seattle.

(continued)

Now write a summary of the dodo bird. Be sure to start with a good introductory sentence, include a few facts in the middle, and end with a good conclusion.

_____

_____

_____

_____

_____

_____

_____

_____

_____

_____

_____

_____

_____

_____

_____

Name _____ Date _____

WRITING A GOOD SUMMARY 2

Read and highlight the following passage.

BILL COSBY

Bill Cosby can do all sorts of things. He is a great comedian and a famous actor. He writes books, does TV commercials and is a great tennis player.

But of all his accomplishments, Bill is most proud of the Fat Albert shows. The Fat Albert shows are not just enjoyable to watch on TV, they help you learn something, too. Bill believes that "nothing is really hard to learn if you have someone to explain it to you."

Bill should know. He grew up in the ghetto in Philadelphia, and worked his way up from there to become a star. After he was famous, he even went back to school and got a doctoral degree in education. Bill wanted to do that because he believes in education.

He is especially interested in the education of poor children. He hopes that Fat Albert can teach youngsters that learning is a good thing and it can even be a pleasure.

Passage and drawing are from *Amazing Animal Stories* 4.5. Copyright © 1979 Turman Publishing Co. Used with permission of Turman Publishing Co., Seattle.

(continued)

Write summary here.

_____

_____

_____

_____

_____

_____

_____

_____

_____

_____

_____

_____

_____

_____

_____

Did you use a good introductory sentence? _____

Did you include important facts? _____

Did you end with a good concluding sentence? _____

Name _____ Date _____

STUDENT ACTIVITY 67

OUTLINE OF YOUR LIFE

You are going to write a five-paragraph report describing yourself. Use the following chart to help you get organized before writing.

I. Introduction

   A. Name _____

   B. Age _____

   C. What do you do? _____

   D. What do you like? _____

   E. Family _____

II. Preschool Years

   A. Born where and when _____

   B. Preschool experience _____

   C. New family members _____

   D. Pets _____

   E. Things you liked _____

   F. Important events or trips _____

(continued)

III. School Years

    A. Important teachers _____

    B. Friends _____

    C. Things you like to do now _____

    D. Things you are good at _____

IV. Future Dreams

    A. What do you want to do as an adult? _____

    B. What type of family would you like to have? _____

    C. Pets? _____

    D. Things to do for fun? _____

    E. Travel?_____

V. Concluding Paragraph

    A. How do you feel about your life so far? _____

    B. What changes would you like to make? _____

Name _____   Date _____

STUDENT ACTIVITY 68

TRANSITION WORDS

Before writing your report of your life, look over the following list of transition words. Use these words to help you change to a new topic. Don't start a sentence with words such as *and*. Use transition words.

Transition Words

after	therefore	again
next	now	also
then	last	another
finally	presently	more
before	to sum it up	one reason
since	even though	for one thing
in summary	first	while
during	for example	earlier
still		

Name _____   Date _____

STUDENT ACTIVITY **69**

EDITING CHECKLIST

1. Write your report using Student Activity 67 as an outline. Cross out items as you include them in your report.

2. Use this editing checklist when you finish:

   a. Did you write a good introductory paragraph that makes the reader want to learn more about you?_____

   b. Did you write three good middle paragraphs? _____

   c. Did you use good descriptive words to make your story interesting? _____

   d. Did you use transition words? _____

   e. Is your last paragraph a good summary that brings the paper to a nice end? _____

   f. Is the paper clear and interesting? _____

   g. Did you write neatly? _____

   h. Did you indent each paragraph? _____

   i. Are all words spelled correctly? _____

   j. Do all sentences end with punctuation marks?_____

   k. Did you capitalize all words that should be capitalized? _____

   l. Do you like this report? _____

Name _____ Date _____

STUDENT ACTIVITY 70

MAP OF A FAMOUS PERSON

On the next page, create a map of a famous person.

1. Write that person's name in the oval at the top of the page.
2. Under the "Background information" oval, write things about this person that occurred in the past.
3. Under the next oval, list the reasons this person is famous.
4. Under the last oval, list the feelings you have about this person.
5. Now write a four-paragraph report. Paragraph 1 should introduce why you chose this person. Paragraph 2 should contain background information. Paragraph 3 should explain why this person is famous, and the last paragraph should conclude your report and explain how you feel about the person.

(continued)

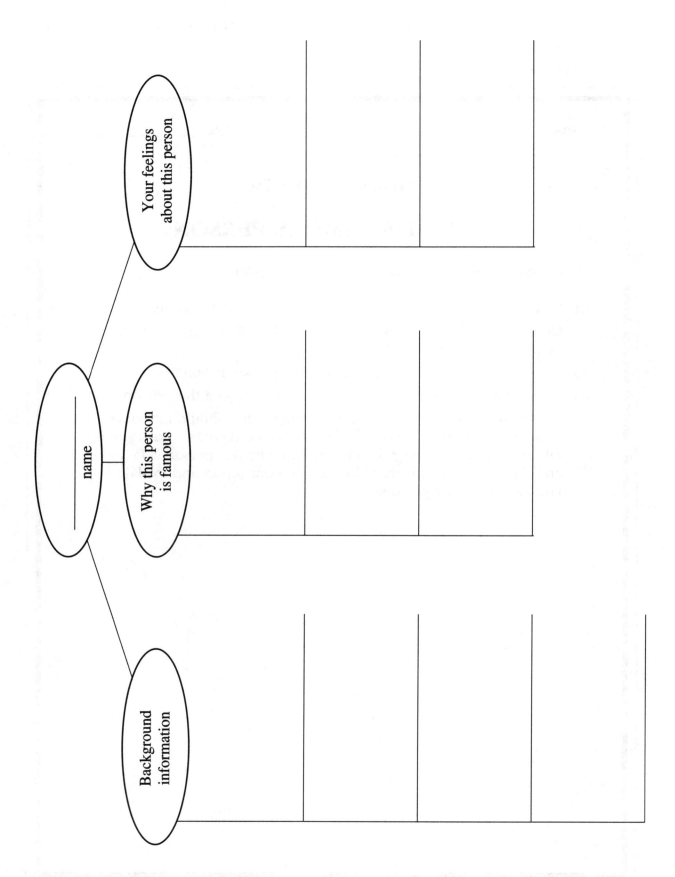

Name _____   Date _____

STUDENT ACTIVITY 71

EDITING CHECKLIST

1. Did you write a good introductory paragraph that makes the reader want to learn more about your topic? _____

2. Did you write good middle paragraphs? _____

3. Did you use good descriptive words to make your paper interesting? _____

4. Did you use transition words? _____

5. Is your last paragraph a good summary that brings the paper to a nice end? _____

6. Is the paper clear and interesting? _____

7. Did you write neatly? _____

8. Did you indent each paragraph? _____

9. Are all words spelled correctly? _____

10. Do all sentences end with punctuation marks? _____

11. Did you capitalize all words that should be capitalized? _____

12. Do you like your report? _____

Name _____ Date _____

ESSAY TERMS

List: make a simple list of what is asked for
State: briefly discuss a main point
Explain or Describe: discuss a main point in more detail than listing or stating
Diagram: use a drawing or chart to answer the question
Compare/Contrast: point out similarities and differences
Summarize: sum up an idea briefly
Define: give a definition

Use your science textbook and make up four of your own essay questions using some of the above terms.

1. _____

   _____

   _____

2. _____

   _____

   _____

3. _____

   _____

   _____

4. _____

   _____

   _____

Name _____ Date _____

STUDENT ACTIVITY 73

PRACTICE WITH ESSAY TERMS

Before you can answer a question correctly, you must first understand exactly what the question asks. The best way to do this is to read the question carefully, circle key essay terms, and underline key words to write about. Try this in the following sentences. The first one is done for you.

1. (List) the three parts of the human circulatory system.
2. State what heat is.
3. Name and describe the four violent storm systems.
4. Explain the three states that water can take, and the temperature for each state.
5. Describe four landforms found in the United States.
6. Diagram the water cycle.
7. Explain what latitude is.
8. Explain three ways Matt demonstrated courage in *The Sign of the Beaver.*
9. Compare and contrast plant cells and animal cells.
10. Summarize the events that led to the Revolutionary War.
11. Define what the term photosynthesis means.

Name _____ Date _____

STUDENT ACTIVITY 74

HOW TO WRITE A GOOD ANSWER TO AN ESSAY QUESTION

1. Read the question carefully.
2. Circle key essay terms and underline key words to write about.
3. Make a brief list, chart, or map of ideas to include.
4. Write a good introductory sentence or paragraph. (Assume that the reader is someone who knows nothing about the subject.)
5. Write the body of the paragraph or report using good descriptive words and transition words.
6. End the paragraph or report with a good concluding statement or paragraph.
7. Read the question again.
8. Read the paragraph and be sure you have answered the question.
9. Edit your work. Point to each word as you read to be sure you didn't leave a word out. Look for punctuation, capitalization, and spelling errors.

LEARN THESE STEPS!

Name _____ Date _____

STUDENT ACTIVITY 75

REVIEW OF ESSAY WRITING STEPS

Fill in the blanks:

1. Read the _____ carefully.

2. Circle _____ essay terms and underline key words to write about.

3. Make a brief list, chart, or map of _____ to include.

4. Write a good _____ sentence or paragraph. (Assume that the reader is someone who knows nothing about the subject.)

5. Write the body of the paragraph or report using good

   _____ words and transition words.

6. End the paragraph or report with a good _____ statement or paragraph.

7. Read the _____ again.

8. Read the paragraph and be sure you have answered the _____

   _____.

9. _____ your work. Point to each word as you read to be sure you didn't leave a word out. Look for punctuation, capitalization, and spelling words.

Name _____   Date _____

STUDENT ACTIVITY **76**

ANSWERING GOOD ESSAY QUESTIONS 1

Read the passage.

TERMITES

Termites are best known for what they destroy. They eat wood. That means they eat tasty things like houses, apartment buildings, and telephone poles.

But termites are builders, too. In fact, they are the best home builders in the animal world. The homes are like anthills, only bigger. Those in Africa may get as high as your house—20 feet. If termites were the size of people, their homes would be huge. The biggest ones would be four times as high as the Empire State Building! And termites can build their homes overnight.

Termites make their homes out of wood mixed with sand and clay. The walls are so strong. It takes an axe to break them. Millions of termites live inside. Each one is busy. There are walls to be fixed, food to find. And the queen is busy laying eggs to make more termites. She can lay eggs really fast—one per second. No wonder termites need such big homes.

Answer the following essay question.

Describe the termite's home.

Passage and drawing from *Amazing Animal Stories 3*. Copyright © 1980 Turman Publishing Co. Used with permission of Turman Publishing Co., Seattle.

1. Read the question and circle the key essay terms and underline key words to write about.

2. Make a brief list, chart, or map of ideas to include in your paragraph.

   _____

   _____

   _____

   _____

3. Write your answer. Use a good beginning, middle, and end. Also, use good descriptive words.

   _____

   _____

   _____

   _____

   _____

   _____

   _____

4. Read over the question. Did you answer it? _____

5. Did you use a good introductory sentence and concluding sentence? _____

6. Edit your paragraph.
   a. Did you indent? _____
   b. Are all words spelled correctly? _____
   c. Is it neat? _____
   d. Did you end every sentence with punctuation? _____
   e. Did you capitalize correctly? _____
   f. Is it clear and easy to understand? _____

Name _____ Date _____

STUDENT ACTIVITY **77**

ANSWERING GOOD ESSAY QUESTIONS 2

Read the passage.

QUICKSAND

Have you ever walked on a beach or in a swamp and felt your feet sinking into a quicksand bog? If you have, you saw the sand cover your shoes. Then it was over your knees. And still you sank deeper into the earth. Chances are you moved about quickly to try to pull yourself free. Your feet caused suction when you struggled. It seemed to you that the quicksand was pulling you down.

There are people who think that quicksand is a mysterious kind of sand. They think it will suck them down below the surface of the bog. This is not true. When people try to pull their feet up out of quicksand, they create a vacuum. This happens because there is not enough air in the wet sand to take the place of their feet when they try to pull them up. So their feet are held in place. They start to panic and fight. They get the false idea that they are being sucked down. But their feet are just being held.

Quicksand is a layer of fine sand floating on water. The water is moving upward from a spring below. The water moves very slowly. But it moves enough to lift the grains of sand a little. This makes them quick or moving.

The sand in quicksand is the same kind of sand you see on beaches. But it is held up by water pressure. It will not suck you down. In fact, it may even lift you up. Scientists agree that quicksand, because it is thicker than water, will hold a lot more weight than water will. You can even float in it just as you can float in a swimming pool.

Quicksand is found in many parts of the United States and Canada. It is wise to learn how to watch for patches of sandy soil that might be quicksand.

The passage is from "Quicksand" in *Essential Skills: Book 1* by Walter Pauk. Copyright © 1982 by Jamestown Publishers, Providence, Rhode Island. Reprinted by permission.

Essay Question

Explain what quicksand is and what happens when a person steps in it.

1. Read the question and circle key essay terms and underline key words to write about.
2. Make brief notes on another sheet of paper.
3. Write your answer on another sheet of paper.
4. Read over the question. Did you answer all parts? ____
5. Did you use a good introductory sentence? ____
6. Did you use descriptive words? ____
7. Did you write a good ending sentence? ____
8. Edit your paragraph.
   a. Did you indent? ____
   b. Are all words spelled correctly? ____
   c. Is it neat? ____
   d. Did you end every sentence with punctuation? ____
   e. Did you capitalize when needed? ____
   f. Is it clear and easy to understand? ____

Chapter
10
Taking Tests

Overview

When students are taught specific strategies for taking tests, they improve their ability to perform well on tests. Students improve memory and vocabulary knowledge by integrating new information with what they already know.

Elliott had put it off long enough. He simply had to sit down and study for his social studies test on Indians. He knew the test was going to include matching, multiple-choice, and true-false questions. Elliott had taken notes on the chapter using the Cornell Method. So, reviewing the key concepts was simple. He knew most of the material, but what would he have to do on the test to demonstrate what he had learned?

First, he figured that the vocabulary words might be put in the matching section. So, Elliott learned the words and their meanings. Then, he thought that the facts about the different tribes might be put in either a multiple-choice or true-false format. He also studied the main ideas about Indians, such as when and how they lived, to help him with the whole test. After about an hour of reviewing for the test, Elliott felt confident that he knew enough about Indians to do well on the test.

Tests are a part of life in school. They are given for a number of reasons: (1) teachers want to know how much students have learned after a unit of study, (2) teachers want to evaluate how effective their lessons have been, (3) teachers, administrators, and parents want to compare students with other students, (4) school personnel want to diagnose the needs of particular students, and (5) students want to know how well they are doing (Devine, 1987). Generally, students do not know how to take tests effectively, but they can learn. In fact, some students earn lower scores on tests simply because they lack "test-wiseness."

Test scores are dependent on many factors, such as the background of the student as well as his or her attitudes, motivations, interests, and reading comprehension abilities. All of these factors being equal (which they never are), test-taking skills can help students reflect what they really know. In this chapter, teaching test-taking skills, improving memory, and taking vocabulary tests will be discussed.

TEACHING TEST-TAKING SKILLS

Students are adept at taking tests when they can apply skills and strategies, unrelated to the content of the test, that increase their scores (Koenke, 1988). These skills and strategies have been found to improve student scores on tests for middle and high school students (Ritter & Idol-Maestas, 1986). However, after reviewing 24 studies, Scruggs, White, and Bennion (1986) concluded that although instructional programs on test-wiseness for elementary school students do not significantly raise achievement test scores, this instruction does help students show less anxiety, more positive self-concepts, and more positive attitudes toward tests. As with other strategies, such as summarizing, middle school seems be the appropriate time to launch a full-scale instructional program in test-wiseness. Much can be done, however, in the elementary grades to help students become more aware and positive about the different forms of tests. Just as sensitivity to text structure helps students comprehend better, sensitivity to test type can help students answer questions more appropriately.

Besides essay tests, which we discussed in the previous chapter, four types of tests are generally given in school: true-false, multiple-choice, matching, and fill-in-the-blank tests. Teachers generally do not use true-false questions as much as other forms of tests (Fleming & Chambers, 1983). However, true-false tests, when properly constructed, can discriminate learning from nonlearning. General guidelines include watching out for words such as *all, never,* or *always* that tend to make statements false, and words such as *sometimes, seldom,* and *generally* that tend to make statements true.

Multiple-choice tests contain a question or statement (stem) and a list of responses (one correct answer and distracters). Guidelines for taking multiple-choice tests include eliminating answers that are blatantly incorrect or "don't fit." Matching tests are generally presented in two columns and are actually composed of several multiple-choice items. Fill-in-the-blank tests (also called completion tests) generally require students to complete a statement with names, dates, symbols, or correct words. Guidelines include reading the entire test before deciding on completing blank spaces.

Helping students understand the different forms of tests can help them be better prepared to answer the questions. In addition, talking about the purpose of tests and test taking is helpful. Students should have the opportunity to make their own tests and make decisions about the best form for assessing certain types of information. That is, students may realize that matching is a good format for assessing key concepts or that multiple choice is ideal for recalling facts. Along with student-generated tests, systematic review sessions should precede each test.

IMPROVING MEMORY

Students are generally asked to *recall* information by identifying the correct answer, correctly matching stimulus with response, or coming up with the right word to complete a sentence. At times, teachers may wish to call on *recognition* to assess whether a student read a book or watched a movie. Recognition is different from recall in that students merely need to demonstrate that they have met the tested item before. Recalling information involves relating new information to something already known and retrieving it later.

Information and ideas go from the "short term memory sensory storage state to short term memory and then to long term memory. The problem is getting it out" (Devine, 1987, p. 293). Memory is not comprised of isolated bits of unrelated facts, ideas, and images, but rather information is stored into larger contexts. New learning is always related to what is already known.

Schema theory has been discussed throughout this book. How information is stored in a person's schema can aid or hinder how it is retrieved. Prereading and prelistening strategies are important for all learners to build background information and activate schema. Then, new information can be stored by relating it to existing schema. Retrieval then becomes more efficient.

Students can improve their memory by integrating new information with known information. They can also employ such devices as mnemonics, mental imagery, association, self-recitation, and relating. All of these strategies for improving memory involve storing information in an organized way for efficient retrieval. Additionally, the more that students personalize information through discussions, stories, or other methods of creating interest, the more likely they are to remember it.

TAKING VOCABULARY TESTS

New research on the teaching of vocabulary has guided recommendations for developing vocabulary knowledge (for recent reviews of research, see Irvin, 1990; Nagy, 1988). Educators commonly accept the fact that students who know many words generally are better readers and perform better on achievement and intelligence tests. Therefore, the direct teaching and assessment of vocabulary in school is essential.

Most research confirms that words must be integrated with schema for them to be learned and used. Looking up words in a dictionary or glossary and writing down the definitions does not generally lead to deep processing and learning of words. The more that students can read, write, listen, speak, integrate, and think about new vocabulary words, the more likely they are to remember those words.

Assessment of vocabulary knowledge can take many forms. Beck and McKeown (1983) developed activities in which students described a situation involving a word (e.g., "Tell me about something you might want to *eavesdrop* on" or "Describe the most *melodious* sound you can think of"). When studying China, one teacher presented this question to her students: "Could a *nomad* be a *mandarin?*" She then asked students to match the following words by drawing lines:

a. read   1. millet

b. ride   2. jade

c. eat on   3. chariot

d. wear   4. pictograph

e. eat   5. porcelain

When preparing for a vocabulary test, students should find the word in context, such as in a science textbook or a story. They should read the paragraph and note how the word is used in the sentence. They can then use the dictionary or glossary to write down the definition of the word using divided page format and perhaps a sample sentence. Students should make additional notes if they can relate the word to their own experiences.

SUMMARY

Tests are given throughout a student's career for many reasons, and students can be taught to improve their ability to perform well on tests. Memory and vocabulary knowledge can also be improved by helping students understand ways of integrating new information and words with known information.

SUGGESTED CLASSROOM ACTIVITIES

═══ GOAL ═══

1. Develop objective test-taking skills by:
   a. Improving memory
   b. Understanding the types of test questions
   c. Understanding test question format
   d. Learning how to take objective tests

Week 15

1. Pass out Student Activity 78, *Improving Concentration.* Have students work on this sheet independently. When finished, let them share in pairs, then discuss concepts as a group. Stress the ways to improve concentration. File the handout in the Study Skills Notebooks.

   Answer Key for Student Activity 78:

   1. (Answers will vary)

   2. (Answers will vary)

   3. Divided page, Cornell Method, charts, mapping

   4. Reciting/writing

   5. Breaks

2. Pass out Student Activity Sheet 79, *Increasing Memory.* Go over as a class. Tell students to study this page in pairs using the Cornell Method, as they will have a test on this tomorrow.

3. Pass out Student Activity 80, *Review of Memory Aids.* Give as a test or let students fill out in pairs. Hand back when graded and be sure all students correct any wrong answers.

4. Teach mnemonics by using Student Activity 81, *Practice with Mnemonics.*

5. Pass out Student Activity 82, *Types of Questions.* Read over and discuss the four types of questions. Independently, have students fill out the bottom half of the sheet. Review answers.

6. Hand out Student Activity Sheet 83, *What Type of Question? 1.* Have students:

   a. Read the passages and highlight the main ideas.

   b. Draw the shape of each paragraph out to the side.

c. Answer the questions.

d. Label the questions as main idea, fact, think about it, or vocabulary.

Review together, using the answer key.

Answer Key for Student Activity 83:

1. b—main idea

2. a—fact

3. d—think about it

4. c—fact

5. a—vocabulary

Paragraph 1 main idea: Life in the wild dog pack is very peaceful.

Paragraph 2 main idea: This dividing of the work is unusual for mammals.

Paragraph 3 main idea: Wild dogs are good hunters.

Paragraph 4 main idea: They run up and take over the whole carcass.

7. Complete Student Activity 84, *What Type of Question? 2,* for extra practice.

Answer Key for Student Activity 84:

1. a—main idea

2. b—fact

3. c—fact

4. c—think about it

Week 16

8. As a class, go over Student Activity 85, *Multiple-Choice Steps,* and file in the Study Skills Notebooks. Then have students independently complete Student Activity 86, *Multiple-Choice Practice.* Review as a class.

Answer Key for Student Activity 86:

1. d—fact

2. a—vocabulary

3. b—main idea or think about it

4. a—fact

9. As a class, go over Student Activity 87, *Answering True-False Questions,* and complete examples independently. Review as a class and file in the Study Skills Notebooks.

Answer Key for Student Activity 87:

A—false; not all turtles live in the the sea; some live on land

B—true; some live by the sea

C—true; we should always eat good food

D—false; not always, not if rotten or sprayed with poison

E—false; not always, mapping or charting may be better

F—false; always edit your essay

10. As a class, go over and complete Student Activity 88, *Completion and Matching*. File in the Study Skills Notebooks.

Answer Key for Student Activity 88:

Completion

1. Christopher Columbus

2. living, swimming

3. ant

Matching

1. D

2. E

3. F

4. B

5. A

6. C

11. As a class, go over and complete Student Activity 89, *Vocabulary Tests*. File in the Study Skills Notebooks.

Answer Key for Student Activity 89:

Group 1: invertebrate/vertebrate

Group 2: fish/gills/fins/scales

Group 3: amphibians/tadpoles/frogs/metamorphosis

12. As a class, go over and complete Student Activity 90, *Spelling Tests*. File in the Study Skills Notebooks.

Answer Key for Student Activity 90:

short i	*long a*	*ing words*
if	came	doing
big	name	going

dig	same	seeing
pig	gate	feeding
did	gave	keeping

13. Pass out Student Activity 91, *Taking an Objective Test.* Read over together. In pairs, have students fold the paper over so they can see only the key words. Have the students quiz each other. File in the Study Skills Notebooks. Let students know that a test on this handout will follow.

14. Have students take the test, Student Activity 92, *Review of Test Taking.* Grade and have students correct all wrong answers.

    Answer Key to Student Activity 92:

      I. (Refer to Student Activity 91)

     II. A. main idea

         B. fact

         C. think about it

         D. vocabulary

    III. A. multiple choice

         B. true/false

         C. completion

         D. matching

     IV. A. set goals

         B. organized information

         C. personalized information

         D. recite

         E. mental imagery

         F. mnemonics

         G. write

         H. review

15. As a final activity, pass out the *Study Skills Coat of Arms* (Student Activity 93). Discuss that a Coat of Arms represented important ideas for families during the past and that some families still use a Coat of Arms as a symbol of their family. This Coat of Arms will represent good study skill techniques. As a class, brainstorm things to list in each of the four categories. Let students choose the most important ideas to them to write in the Coat of Arms.

Answer Key for Student Activity 93:

At home

1. quiet place

2. necessary supplies

3. set aside time to study

4. take breaks

5. review notes

6. set goals

At school

1. read actively

2. listen actively

3. find meanings of new words

4. ask questions

5. try hard

6. keep desk organized

7. use assignment pad

8. use monthly calendar

Goals

(Answers will vary)

Tools

1. highlighting

2. SQ3R

3. TQLR

4. mnemonics

5. concentrate

6. mapping

7. Cornell Notetaking

8. paragraph structure

9. paragraph purpose

Name _____   Date _____

STUDENT ACTIVITY 78

IMPROVING CONCENTRATION

Increasing concentration increases memory.

1. List five things that can interfere with concentration when studying and list solutions to improve concentration. The first one is done for you.

    Problems when Studying   *Solutions*

    a. <u>distracted by TV</u>   <u>turn it off/leave room</u>

    b. _____   _____

    c. _____   _____

    d. _____   _____

    e. _____   _____

2. Concentration is something you can control by wanting to learn and setting goals. Decide on three goals for this coming week and really concentrate on meeting these goals.

    a. _____

    b. _____

    c. _____

3. Concentration can also be increased by good note-taking. List three different ways to take notes.

   a. _____

   b. _____

   c. _____

4. One of the best ways to improve concentration is to recite information. Next time you are studying for a test, try saying the facts out loud and see if this helps you remember. Writing information also improves concentration. What are the two ways to improve concentration?

   a. _____

   b. _____

5. When you get tired, take breaks. A tired brain cannot concentrate or remember well. When you get tired, take _____.

Name _____ Date _____

STUDENT ACTIVITY 79

INCREASING MEMORY

To remember more things for a longer time, we must get information from short-term memory to long-term memory. Short-term memory is where we store information in our brain that we do not need to remember, such as what we had for dinner. Long-term memory is where we store information in our brain that we need for a long time, such as our teacher's name, where we live, and the material that will be on the next test at school.

Good students know how to get information from short-term memory to long-term memory. Following are some of the techniques good students use:

Concentrate | Think deeply about the material you are to learn. Get away from distractions. Example: Study in a quiet place and think about the material.

Set Goals | Decide what you are going to do, what grade you want on the next test, and how long you will study. Example: I want an A on this science test about mammals. I will study for one hour and take two breaks.

Organize Information | Use maps, Cornell Notetaking Method, charts, divided page, or highlighting to organize information into main ideas and supporting details. We remember more information if it is grouped into related units. Example: I will use a map to organize the characteristics of mammals.

Personalize Information	Relate what you are learning to what you already know. Example: I know I am a mammal, so I can remember the characteristics. All mammals have hair or fur; I have hair. All mammals give birth to live animals; I did not hatch from an egg, and so on.
Recite Information	Say the material out loud to yourself, covering up the map you made. Example: I will say out loud what I think is on the map and then check with the map.
Use Mental Imagery	Visualize your teacher talking about the material, or visualize the film you saw or pictures in the textbook. Example: I remember the picture of the mother dog nursing her puppies. This helps me remember that all mammals nurse their young.
Use Mnemonics	Use the first letter of a word to remember lists. Example: Characteristics of mammals: Five Little Brown Worms Nap—Fur, Live Births, Warm Blooded, Nurse their young.
Write Information	Any information that you continue to forget should be written down several times. Example: I can't remember how many types of mammals there are. I need to write this down.
Review	Leave time to review information after studying. Example: I will study on Tuesday and review on Wednesday for the test on Thursday.

Name _____ Date _____

STUDENT ACTIVITY 80

REVIEW OF MEMORY AIDS

Study Student Activity 79. Notice that it is arranged in the divided page format. Fold the paper over and learn each technique. Now take the following study skills test without looking back at your notes.

Concentrate means _____

_____

_____

Set Goals means _____

_____

_____

Organize Information means _____

_____

_____

Personalize Information means _____

_____

_____

Recite Information means _____

_____

_____

Use Mental Imagery means_____

_____

_____

Use Mnemonics means _____

_____

_____

Write Information means_____

_____

_____

Review means_____

_____

_____

Name _____ Date _____

PRACTICE WITH MNEMONICS

Mnemonics are memory aids, such as SQ3R. Using initials helps you remember Survey, Question, Read, Recite, Review. A very common mnemonic is used to learn the names and order of notes on the lines of a treble clef staff: Every Good Boy Does Fine (EGBDF). Create your own mnemonics to help you remember the following:

1. The four violent storm groups: hurricanes, tornadoes, thunderstorms, blizzards. (Use initials and arrange in any order).

   _____

   _____

2. The names of the first six presidents of the United States: Washington, Adams, Jefferson, Madison, Monroe, Adams.

   _____

   _____

3. The names of the original 13 colonies: Virginia, Massachusetts, New Hampshire, New York, Connecticut, Maryland, Rhode Island, Delaware, Pennsylvania, North Carolina, New Jersey, South Carolina, Georgia.

   _____

   _____

4. Using one of your textbooks, make your own mnemonics for lists of items to remember.

   _____

   _____

Name _____ Date _____

TYPES OF QUESTIONS

There are four basic types of questions. As you answer questions, keep in mind the type of question it is so you can pick the best answer. Do not answer a main idea question as though it is a fact question.

1. *Main idea:* What is the main point of the passage?
2. *Fact:* This is a detail that can be found in the passage.
3. *Think about it (inferred or implied):* The answer is not directly stated in the passage. You must think about the question and decide based on the information in the passage. Do not answer this type of question with your own opinion unless the question asks for your opinion. Usually, the questions want the author's opinion. Questions often start with: *According to the author* or *This passage implies*, and the like.
4. *Vocabulary:* These questions test your understanding of a word or phrase mentioned in the passage. Words in the English language can have many different meanings, so be sure that you know how the word was used in the passage.

(continued)

From memory, list the four types of questions here with a brief description.

1. _____   _____

   _____

   _____

2. _____   _____

   _____

   _____

3. _____   _____

   _____

   _____

4. _____   _____

   _____

   _____

Name _____ Date _____

WHAT TYPE OF QUESTION ? 1

Read the following passage. Answer the questions and decide what type of question it is.

WILD DOGS

Life in the wild dog pack is very peaceful. There is no fighting between the dogs, no matter how many share the kill. Sometimes a lame or sick dog arrives too late for the meal. It must beg for food from one or more pack members. Some of the dogs will then share the meat they have already eaten by throwing up some of it for their hungry friend.

Once a year, a female in the pack has pups. There may be as many as 16 in a litter. The pack finds a den—often an empty hyena burrow—in which the pups are born. Here, they stay until the pups are three to four months old and are able to travel with the pack. The pack usually goes hunting at dawn or sometimes in the late evening. During this time, several dogs stay behind and guard the pups. This dividing of the work is unusual in mammals.

Wild dogs are good hunters. They usually do not return without having killed. When they return to the den, they feed not only the pups but also the guards by throwing up chunks of meat carried home in their stomachs.

When the pups are old enough to travel, they trail behind the hunting pack. After a kill has been made, they run up and take over the whole carcass. They eat until they are full, while the adults wait for any scraps that may be left. Often, nothing is left when the pups are done and the pack must hunt again.

(continued)

1. This passage talks about the wild dog as:

    a. a selfish animal.

    b. a parent and hunter.

    c. a species that is dying out.

    d. an enemy of humans.

    Type of question:_____

2. Female dogs often give birth in

    a. empty hyena burrows.

    b. small underground caves.

    c. thick bushes.

    d. hollow tree trunks.

    Type of question:_____

3. The wild dog seems to be

    a. full of revenge and anger.

    b. uninterested in caring for its family.

    c. mean and ill tempered.

    d. a loyal member of the pack.

    Type of question:_____

4. The last paragraph describes the pack's

    a. mating habits.

    b. size.

    c. eating habits.

    d. leader.

    Type of question:_____

5. As used in this passage, a carcass is

    a. the body of a dead animal.

    b. a wounded dog.

    c. a young dog.

    d. the entire wild dog pack.

    Type of question:_____

The passage and five questions are from "Working Together" in *Essential Skills: Book 5* by Walter Pauk. Copyright © 1982 by Jamestown Publishers, Providence, Rhode Island. Reprinted by permission.

Name _____ Date _____

STUDENT ACTIVITY 84

WHAT TYPE OF QUESTION ? 2

Read the following passage. Answer each question and decide what type of question it is.

THICK-KNEE BIRD

Some animals really pick strange friends. The thick-knee bird is a good example. This is a little bird with thick joints on its long legs. (That's why it's called the thick-knee bird. Actually, the joints are its ankles.) It lives on the Nile River and it is friends with the deadly Nile Crocodile. Every year, about 1,000 people are killed by the crocodile. But crocodiles never hurt their buddies, the thick-knee birds. They even let these birds walk right inside their mouths. The birds eat the leeches that can get in the crocodile's mouth and drink the crocodile's blood. If danger is coming, thick-knee birds warn the crocodiles with their cries. The first person to write this down was a man from Greece. He lived 2,500 years ago. When he told people what he saw, no one believed him. Now, we know that it is true. Even crocodiles have to have some friends.

(continued)

1. The main idea of the story is

    a. how the thick-knee bird is friends with the crocodile.

    b. how crocodiles kill people.

    c. how thick-knee birds run on long legs.

    Type of question:_____

2. The thick joints on this bird's legs are its

    a. knees.

    b. ankles.

    c. hips.

    Type of question:_____

3. Thick-knee birds go in crocodiles' mouths and eat

    a. teeth.

    b. blood.

    c. leeches.

    Type of question:_____

4. You might say

    a. thick-knee birds help only crocodiles.

    b. crocodiles help only thick-knee birds.

    c. crocodiles and thick-knee birds help each other.

    Type of question:_____

Name _____ Date _____

STUDENT ACTIVITY 85

MULTIPLE-CHOICE STEPS

Learn these steps for answering multiple-choice questions.

1. Read the question.
2. Decide what type of question it is: fact, main idea, vocabulary, or think about it.
3. Decide what you think the answer is before reading the choices.
4. Read all the choices before answering the question.
5. Make the best choice by eliminating choices you know are wrong.
6. Read the question again, this time with the answer you chose to see if it sounds right.

Example: Octopus live in......

1. Read the question.
2. What type of question is it? _____
3. What is the answer? _____
4. Now read all of the choices to find the answer you want.
   a. rivers
   b. lakes
   c. oceans
   d. rivers and lakes

Eliminate the wrong choices and pick the one you were looking for. Now go back and read the question again and the correct answer to see that it fits. Octopus live in oceans.

Name _____ Date _____

MULTIPLE-CHOICE PRACTICE

Now answer the following questions using the steps you just learned.

1. Question: Who was the first president of the United States?

   What type of question is this? _____

   What do you think is the answer? _____

   Now read all the choices.

   Choices:
   a. Abraham Lincoln
   b. Ulysses S. Grant
   c. Neal Armstrong
   d. George Washington

Circle the best choice. Reread the question and be sure your answer fits.

2. Question: If something is huge, it is....

   What type of question is this? _____

   What do you think is the answer?_____

   Now read all the choices.

   Choices:
   a. Very large
   b. Large
   c. Small
   d. Tiny

Circle the best answer. Reread the question and be sure your answer fits.

3. Question: The lesson to be learned from Little Red Riding Hood is . . . .

   What type of question is this? _____

   What do you think is the answer? _____

   Now read the choices.

   Choices:

   a. Wolves can be mean

   b. Don't talk to strangers

   c. Wearing red can be dangerous

   d. Grandmothers are weak

Circle the best answer. Reread the question and be sure your answer fits.

4. Question: Who discovered America?

   What type of question is this? _____

   What do you think is the answer? _____

   Now read the choices.

   Choices:

   a. Christopher Columbus

   b. Your teacher

   c. Michael Jordan

   d. Albert Einstein

Circle the best answer. Reread the question and be sure your answer fits.

Name _____ Date _____

ANSWERING TRUE-FALSE QUESTIONS

I. Watch out for words such as *all, always,* and *never.* These words usually make a sentence not correct, or false.

   Example:

   A. All students love to read. (This is false because not *all* love to read.)

   Watch for words such as *sometimes, seldom,* and *generally.* These words usually make a sentence correct, or true.

   Example:

   B. Some students love to read. (Now the sentence is true.)

   Some sentences can still be true even with words like *all, always,* and *never.*

   Example:

   A. Never cross the street without looking both ways. (This is true because there is never a time you should cross the street without looking.)

   B. All fish live in water. (This is true because all fish do live in water.)

II. Read and answer each of the following true-false questions. Explain why the answer is true or false.

   A. All turtles live near or in the sea. (This question is _____

   because: _____

   _____

   _____

B. Some turtles live near or in the sea. (This question is _____

because: _____

_____

_____

C. We should always eat nutritious food. (This question is _____

because: _____

_____

_____

D. Apples are always good to eat. (This question is _____

because: _____

_____

_____

E. You should always use the Cornell Notetaking System when

preparing for science tests. (This question is _____

because: _____

_____

_____

F. Never edit your essay before turning it in. (This question is _____

because: _____

_____

_____

Name _____   Date _____

STUDENT ACTIVITY 88

COMPLETION AND MATCHING

Steps for Completion Questions

1. Read the whole sentence or paragraph.

2. Decide on the word to fit in the blank.

3. Read the whole sentence again with your choice to be sure it fits and sounds correct.

4. If the blank is at the beginning of the sentence, be sure to capitalize the word.

Now try these:

1. _____ _____ discovered America. (Did you write in the first and last name? Did you capitalize the name?)

2. Fish can be found _____ in water. (Did your choice end with *ing?*)

3. An _____ is a small insect that builds homes in the ground by piling dirt up around their home. (You must choose an insect whose name begins with a vowel since the word *an* is used before the blank.)

Steps for Answering Matching Questions

1. Read the directions. Can you use a choice more than once?

2. Quickly scan all choices.

3. Match the easy questions first, crossing off the choices as you use them if they can be used only once.

4. Now go back to the more difficult questions. Make educated guesses.

Now try these. You can only use a choice once.

_____ 1. Divided page

_____ 2. TQLR

_____ 3. Four types of questions

_____ 4. SQ3R

_____ 5. Mnemonics

_____ 6. Three paragraph purposes

A. memory aid

B. survey, question, read, recite, review

C. entertain, main idea, facts

D. key words on one side, definition on the other

E. tune in, question, listen, review

F. fact, think about it, vocabulary, main idea

Name _____ Date _____

STUDENT ACTIVITY 89

VOCABULARY TESTS

Steps for Preparing for Vocabulary Tests

1. Group words together by characteristics (such as all animals or all landforms).

2. Use the divided page format to record words and definitions.

3. Test yourself by folding the paper over so you can only see the vocabulary word. Now recite the definition out loud. Check yourself. Now fold over the paper so you can only see the definition. Say the key word out loud.

4. Highlight any word you continue to miss and review this word many times by rewriting the word and the definition.

Now try this method with the following words:

1. invertebrate   6. fin
2. gills   7. vertebrate
3. amphibian   8. metamorphosis
4. fish   9. scales
5. tadpoles   10. frog

1. Group the words according to characteristics into three groups. The first word of each group is done for you.

Group 1	*Group 2*	*Group 3*
invertebrate	*fish*	*amphibians*

2. Record words in groups using the divided page format. Write the definitions. The first one is done for you.

Key Word	*Definition*
invertebrate	animal without a backbone

3. Test yourself.

4. Highlight words you continue to have difficulty remembering.

Name _____   Date _____

SPELLING TESTS

Steps for Preparing for Spelling Tests

1. Group words together by patterns (by syllables, sounds, or characteristics).

2. Study one group at a time.

3. Use the divided page to practice the word. Write it down while spelling it orally. Fold the paper over as though you were covering up a vocabulary word. Write the word from memory, spelling it orally. Check the word by opening up the paper and comparing it to the first word. Continue this method several times.

4. Take a practice test the night before the test.

5. If you need to, divide your spelling words into study groups. Study a few each night. For example, if you have 20 words to learn, study 7 on Monday night, 7 on Tuesday while reviewing the 7 from Monday, and study the last 6 on Wednesday while reviewing the 14 from Monday and Tuesday. On Thursday review all 20 words.

Now try this method with the following words:

came	seeing	going	did	big
if	dig	name	gave	gate
doing	same	feeding	pig	keeping

1. Divide the words into three groups to study each day.

| *Monday*
(short *i* words)
study 1–5 | *Tuesday*
(long *a* words)
review 1–5
study 6–10 | *Wednesday*
(ending in *ing*)
review 1–10
study 11–15 | *Thursday*
Review all
15 words in
order and out
of order |

1. _____   6. _____   11. _____

2. _____   7. _____   12. _____

3. _____   8. _____   13. _____

4. _____   9. _____   14. _____

5. _____   10. _____   15. _____

2. Study one group at a time by writing it down and saying it orally in the divided page format.

Name _____   Date _____

TAKING AN OBJECTIVE TEST

Relax

1. Take two or three deep breaths and relax.

Budget

2. Budget your time. Survey the whole test so you get an idea of what you will be expected to do.

Directions

3. Read directions carefully and underline key words.

Easy Questions

4. Answer all easy questions first.

Difficult Questions

5. Place a light mark by difficult questions and go back to them after answering all easy questions.

Continue to Relax

6. Take deep breaths.

Reread

7. Look over your test when you finish to double check your answers.

Name _____ Date _____

STUDENT ACTIVITY 92

REVIEW OF TEST TAKING

I. After studying Student Activity 91, explain these techniques:

A. Relax _____

_____

B. Budget _____

_____

C. Directions_____

_____

D. Easy Questions _____

_____

E. Difficult Questions_____

_____

F. Continue to Relax _____

_____

G. Reread_____

_____

(continued)

II. What are the four types of test questions? The first one is listed for you.

A. _Main idea_ _____

B. _____

C. _____

D. _____

III. What are the four common forms of objective test questions? The first one is listed for you.

A. _Multiple choice_ _____

B. _____

C. _____

D. _____

IV. Name four ways to increase memory and concentration. The first one is listed for you.

A. _Set goals_ _____

B. _____

C. _____

D. _____

Name _____ Date _____

STUDENT ACTIVITY 93

STUDY SKILLS COAT OF ARMS

MAKING A DIFFERENCE

Things You Can Do at Home:

1. _____
2. _____
3. _____
4. _____
5. _____
6. _____

Things You Can Do at School:

1. _____
2. _____
3. _____
4. _____
5. _____
6. _____
7. _____
8. _____

Set goals:

Short-term goals:

1. _____
2. _____
3. _____

Long-term goals:

1. _____
2. _____
3. _____

Tools:

1. _____
2. _____
3. _____
4. _____
5. _____
6. _____

References

Anderson, R. C., & Pearson, P. D. (1984). A schema-theoretic view of basic processes in reading. In P. D. Pearson (Ed.), *Handbook of reading research* (pp. 255–292). White Plains, NY: Longman.

Anderson, T. H., & Armbruster, B. B. (1984). Studying. In P. D. Pearson (Ed.), *Handbook of reading research* (pp. 657–680). White Plains, NY: Longman.

Andre, M. D. A., & Anderson, T. H. (1978–79). The development and evaluation of a self-questioning study technique. *Reading Research Quarterly, 14,* 605–623.

Applebee, A. N. (1981). *Writing in the secondary school: English and the content areas.* Urbana, IL: National Council of Teachers of English.

Armbruster, B. B. (1979). *An investigation of the effectiveness of "mapping" text as a studying strategy for middle school students.* Unpublished doctoral dissertation, University of Illinois.

Armbruster, B. B., & Anderson, T. H. (1980). *The effect of mapping on the free recall of expository text* (Technical Report #160). Urbana, IL: Center for the Study of Reading.

Baker, L., & Brown, A. L. (1984). Cognitive monitoring in reading. In J. Flood (Ed.), *Understanding reading comprehension: Cognition, language, and the structure of prose* (pp. 21–44). Newark, DE: International Reading Association.

Bauman, J. F. (1981). Effect of ideational prominence on children's reading comprehension of expository prose. *Journal of Reading Behavior, 13,* 49–56.

Beach, J. A. (1983). Teaching students to write informational reports. *Elementary School Journal, 84,* 213–220.

Beck, I. L., & McKeown, M. G. (1983). Learning words well: A program to enhance vocabulary and comprehension. *Reading Teacher, 39,* 622.

Beck, I. L., Omanson, R. C., & McKeown, M. G. (1982). An instructional redesign of reading lessons: Effects on comprehension. *Reading Research Quarterly, 17*(4), 462–481.

Beyer, B. (1987). *Practical strategies for the teaching of thinking.* Boston: Allyn and Bacon.

Boodt, G. M. (1984). Critical listeners become critical listeners in remedial reading class. *The Reading Teacher, 37,* 390–394.

Brown, A. L. (1978). Knowing when, where, and how to remember: A problem of metacognition. In R. Glaser (Ed.), *Advances in instructional psychology* (pp. 77–165). Hillsdale, NJ: Erlbaum.

Brown, A. L. (1982). Learning how to learn from reading. In J. A. Langer & M. T. Smith-Burke (Eds.), *Reader meets author: Bridging the gap* (pp. 26–54). Newark, DE: International Reading Association.

Brown, A. L., & Day, J. D. (1983). Macrorules for summarizing texts: The development of expertise. *Journal of Verbal Learning and Verbal Behavior, 22,* 1–14.

Brown, A. L., Campione, J. C., & Day, J. D. (1981). Learning to learn: On training students to learn from texts. In J. D. Harris & A. Sipay (Eds.), *Readings on reading instruction* (pp. 317–325). White Plains, NY: Longman.

Brown, A. L., Day, J. D., & Jones, R. S. (1983). The development of plans for summarizing texts. *Child Development, 54,* 968–979.

Caine, R. N., & Caine, G. (1991). *Making connections: Teaching and the human brain.* Alexandria, VA: Association for Supervision and Curriculum Development.

Crawley, S. J., & Mountain, L. H. (1988). *Strategies for guiding content reading.* Boston: Allyn and Bacon.

Davey, B. (1985). Helping readers think beyond print through self-questioning. *Middle School Journal,* 26–27.

Devine, T. G. (1982). *Listening skills schoolwide: Activities and programs.* Urbana, IL: National Council for the Teachers of English.

Devine, T. G. (1987). *Teaching study skills.* Boston: Allyn and Bacon.

DiVesta, F. J., Schultz, C. B., & Dangel, T. R. (1973). Passage organization and imposed learning strategies in comprehension and recall of connected discourse. *Memory and Cognition, 1,* 471–476.

Doctorow, M., Wittrock, M. C., & Marks, C. (1970). Generative processes in reading comprehension. *Journal of Applied Psychology, 70* (2), 109–118.

Dole, J. A., Duffy, G. G., Roehler, L. R., & Pearson, P. D. (1991). Moving from the old to the new: Research on reading comprehension instruction. *Review of Educational Research, 61*(2), 239–264.

Duffy, G. G., & Roehler, L. R. (1986). *Improving classroom reading instruction: A decision-making approach.* New York: Random House.

Duker, S. (1968). *Listening bibliography.* Metuchen, NJ: Scarecrow.

Dupuis, M. M., Lee, J. W., Badiali, B. J., & Askov, E. N. (1989). *Teaching reading and writing in the content areas.* Glenview, IL: Scott, Foresman.

Fisher, C. J., & Terry, C. A. (1990). *Children's language and the language arts: A literature-based approach.* Boston: Allyn and Bacon.

Fitzgerald, J. (1989). Research on stories: Implications for teachers. In K. D. Muth (Ed.), *Children's comprehension of text* (pp. 2–36). Newark, DE: International Reading Association.

Fleming, M., & Chambers, B. (1983). Teacher-made tests: Windows on the classroom. In W. E. Hathaway (Ed.), *New directions for testing and measurement: Volume 19: Testing in the schools* (pp. 29–38). San Francisco: Jossey-Bass.

Gall, M. D., Gall, J. P., Jacobsen, D. R., & Bullock, T. L. (1990). *Tools for learning: A guide to teaching study skills.* Alexandria, VA: Association for Supervision and Curriculum Development.

Garner, R. (1992). Metacognition and self-monitoring strategies. In S. J. Samuels & A. E. Farstrup (Eds.), *What research has to say about reading instruction* (pp. 236–252). Newark, DE: International Reading Association.

Gillet, J. W., & Temple, C. (1990). *Understanding reading problems: Assessment and instruction.* Glenview, IL: Scott, Foresman.

Gillis, M. K., & Olson, M. W. (1987). Elementary IRIs: Do they reflect what we know about text type/structure and comprehension? *Reading Research and Instruction, 1,* 36–44.

Harris, A. J., & Sipay, E. R. (1985). *How to increase reading ability: A guide to developmental and remedial methods* (8th ed.). New York: Longman.

Harris, A. J., & Sipay, E. R. (1990). *How to increase reading ability: A guide to developmental and remedial methods* (9th ed.) New York: Longman.

Hartley, J., & Davies, I. K. (1978). Notetaking: A critical review. *Programmed Learning and Educational Technology, 15,* 207–224.

Heimlich, J. E., & Pittelman, S. D. (1986). *Semantic mapping: Classroom applications.* Newark, DE: International Reading Association.

Hidi, S., & Anderson, V. (1986). Producing written summaries: Task demands, cognitive operations, and implications for instruction. *Review of Educational Research, 56*(4), 473–493.

Irvin, J. L. (1990). *Vocabulary knowledge: Guidelines for instruction.* Washington, DC: National Education Association.

Jacobsen, D. R. (1989). *The effects of taking class notes using Cornell Method on students' test performance and notetaking quality.* Unpublished doctoral dissertation, University of Oregon.

Johnston, P. (1985). Instruction and student independence. *The Elementary School Journal, 84* (3), 338–344.

Kiewra, K. (1984). Acquiring effective notetaking skills: An alternative to professional notetaking. *Journal of Reading, 27*(4), 299.

Kiewra, K. A. (1985). Investigating notetaking and review: A depth of processing alternative. *Educational Psychologist, 20,* 23–32.

Koenke, K. (1988). Test-wiseness: Programs and problems. *Journal of Reading, 31,* 480–483.

Langer, J. A. (1986). *Children's reading and writing: Structures and strategies.* Norwood, NJ: Ablex.

Leverentz, F., & Garman, D. (1987). What was that you said? *Instructor, 96,* 66–70.

Lunsteen, S. W. (1979). *Listening: Its impact on reading and the other language arts.* Urbana, IL: National Council for the Teaching of English.

Mason, J. M., & Au, K. H. (1990). *Reading instruction for today.* Glenview, IL: Scott, Foresman.

McAndrew, D. A. (1983). Underlining and notetaking: Some suggestions from research. *Journal of Reading, 27,* 103–108.

McGee, L. M. (1982). The influence of metacognitive knowledge of expository text structure on discourse recall. In J. A. Niles & L. A. Harris (Eds.), *New inquiries in reading: Research and instruction* (pp. 64–70). Rochester, NY: National Reading Conference.

McNeil, J. D., & Donant, L. (1982). Summarization strategy for improving reading comprehension. In J. A. Niles & L. A. Harris (Eds.), *New inquiries in reading research and instruction.* Rochester, NY: National Reading Conference.

McTighe, J., & Lyman, F. T., Jr. (1988). Cueing thinking in the classroom: The promise of theory-embedded tools. *Educational Leadership, 45,* 18–24.

Moore, D. W., Readence, J. E., & Rickelman, R. J. (1989). *Prereading activities for content area reading and learning* (2nd ed.). Newark, DE: International Reading Association.

Nagy, W. E. (1988). *Teaching vocabulary to improve reading comprehension.* Newark, DE: International Reading Association.

Nessel, D. D., Jones, M. B., & Dixon, C. N. (1989). *Thinking through the language arts.* New York: Macmillan.

Newell, G. E., & Winograd, P. (1989). The effects of writing on learning from expository text. *Written Communication, 6* (2), 196–217.

Noyce, R. M., & Christie, J. F. (1989). *Integrating reading and writing instruction in grades K–8.* Boston: Allyn and Bacon.

Ogle, D. M. (1989). The know, want to know, learn strategy. In K. D. Muth (Ed.), *Children's comprehension of text* (pp. 205–223). Newark, DE: International Reading Association.

Palincsar, A. S., & Brown, A. L. (1983). *Reciprocal teaching of comprehension-monitoring activities* (Technical Report No. 269). Champaign, IL: Center for the Study of Reading.

Paris, S. G., Wasik, B. A., & Turner, J. C. (1991). The development of strategic readers. In R. Barr, M. Kamil, P. B. Mosenthal, & P. D. Pearson (Eds.), *Handbook of reading research: Volume II* (pp. 609–640). New York: Longman.

Paris, S. G., Wasik, B. A., & van der Westhuizen, G. (1988). Meta-metacognition: A review of research. In M. W. McLaughlin (Ed.), *Dialogues in literacy research* (pp. 143–166). Chicago National Reading Conference.

Paris, S. G., & Winograd, P. (1990). How metacognition can promote academic learning and instruction. In B. F. Jones & L. Idol (Eds.), *Dimensions of thinking and cognitive instruction* (pp. 15–52). Hillsdale, NY: Erlbaum.

Pauk, W. (1974; 1978; 1984). *How to study in college.* Boston: Houghton Mifflin.

Pearson, P. D. (1985). Changing the face of reading comprehension instruction. *The Reading Teacher, 38,* 724–737.

Pearson, P. D., & Fielding, L. (1984). Research update: Listening comprehension. In A. Harris & E. R. Sipay (Eds.), *Readings on reading instruction* (pp. 74–84). New York: Longman.

Pearson, P. D., & Fielding, L. (1991). Comprehension instruction. In R. Barr, M. Kamil, P. B. Mosenthal, & P. D. Pearson (Eds.), Handbook of reading research: Volume II (pp. 815–860). New York: Longman.

Rickards, J. P. (1984). Notetaking: Theory and research. In A. Harris & E. R. Sipay (Eds.), *Readings on reading instruction* (pp. 331–336). New York: Longman.

Ritter, S., & Idol-Maestas, L. (1986). Teaching middle school students to use a test taking strategy. *Journal of Educational Research, 79,* 350–357.

Robinson, F. P. (1970). *Effective study*. New York: Harper and Brothers.

Scruggs, T. E., White, K. R., & Bennion, K. (1986). Teaching test taking skills to elementary grade students: A meta-analysis. *Elementary School Journal, 87*, 69–82.

Sinatra, R. C., Berg, D., & Dunn, R. (1985). Semantic mapping improves reading comprehension of learning disabled students. *Teaching Exceptional Children, 17*(4), 310–314.

Singer, H., & Donlan, D. (1988). *Reading and learning from text*. Hillsdale, NJ: Erlbaum.

Smith, P. L., & Tompkins, G. E. (1988). Structured notetaking: A new strategy for content area readers. *Journal of Reading, 32*, 46–53.

Stewart, O., & Tei, E. (1983). Some implications of metacognition for reading instruction. *Journal of Reading, 26*, 36–43.

Sticht, T. G., & James, J. H. (1984). Listening and reading. In P. D. Pearson (Ed.), *Handbook of reading research* (pp. 293–318). New York: Longman.

Taylor, B. M. (1980). Children's memory for expository text after reading. *Reading Research Quarterly, 15*, 399–411.

Taylor, B. M. (1982). Text structure and children's comprehension and memory for expository material. *Journal of Educational Psychology, 74*, 323–340.

Taylor, B. M. (1986). Teaching middle grade students to summarize content textbook material. In J. F. Bauman (Ed.), *Teaching main idea comprehension* (pp. 195–209). Newark, DE: International Reading Association.

Taylor, B. (1992). Text structure, comprehension, and recall. In S. J. Samuels & A. E. Farstrup (Eds.), *What research has to say about reading instruction* (pp. 220–235). Newark, DE: International Reading Association.

Taylor, K. K. (1986). Summary writing by young children. *Reading Research Quarterly, 21*, 193–208.

Tei, E., & Stewart, O. (1985). Effective studying from text: Applying metacognitive strategies. *Journal for Reading, 16*(2), 46–55.

Temple, C., & Gillet, J. W. (1989). *Language arts learning processes and teaching practices*. Glenview, IL: Scott, Foresman.

Tonjes, M. J. (1991). *Secondary reading, writing, and learning*. Boston: Allyn and Bacon.

Tonjes, M. J., & Zintz, M. V. (1981). *Teaching reading/thinking/study skills in content classrooms*. Dubuque, IA: William C. Brown.

Vacca, R. T., & Vacca, J. L. (1989). *Content area reading*. Glenview, IL: Scott, Foresman.

Vaughn, J. L., & Estes, T. H. (1986). *Reading and reasoning beyond the primary grades*. Boston: Allyn and Bacon.

Winograd, P. N. (1984). Contexts of literacy: Translating research into policy. In T. Raphael (Ed.), *The contexts of school-based literacy* (pp. 271–280). New York: Random House.

Winograd, P. N., & Bridge, C. A. (1986). The Comprehension of important information in written prose. In J. F. Bauman (Ed.), *Teaching main idea comprehension* (pp. 18–48). Newark, DE: International Reading Association.

Index

Anderson, T. H., 2, 52, 74, 77, 128, 148
Anderson, V., 176
Andre, M. D. A., 74
Applebee, A. N., 174
Armbruster, B. B., 2, 77, 128, 148
Askov, K. H., 52
Au, K. H., 14
Auditory learning, 29

Badiali, B. J., 52
Baker, L., 176
Bauman, J. F., 54
Beach, J. A., 179
Beck, I. L., 149, 207
Bennion, K., 205
Berg, D., 148
Beyer, B., 175
Boodt, G. M., 98
Brain-based learning, 128
Bridge, C. A., 54
Brown, A., L., 12, 13, 73, 176
Bulloch, T. L., 127

Caine, G., 128
Caine, R. N., 128
Campione, J. C., 176
Chambers, B., 206
Charts, 128
Checklist, 6–8
Christie, J. F., 176
Cornell Notetaking System, 128
Crawley, S. J., 148
Criterion tasks, 2

Dangle, T. R., 149
Davey, B., 74–75
Davies, I. K., 127
Day, J. D., 176
Demonstrating understanding, 5–6

Devine, T. G., 76, 97, 98, 127, 178, 205, 206
DiVesta, F. J., 149
Dixon, C. N., 178
DLTA, 99
Doctorow, M., 176
Dole, J. A., 11
Donant, L., 176
Donlon, D., 74
Duffy, G. G., 11, 77, 127
Duker, S., 98
Dunn, R., 148
Dupuis, M. M., 52

Essay questions, 173, 175
Estes, T. H., 75
Expository text, 52-54
Extracting information, 4

Fielding, L., 98–99, 149
Fill-in-the-blank questions, 206
Fisher, C. J., 177
Fitzgerald, J., 75
Fleming, M., 206
Flexible reading, 56–57

Gall, J. P., 127
Gall, M. P., 127
Garman, D., 98
Garner, R., 74
Gillet, J. W., 98, 99, 177, 178
Gillis, M. K., 53

Harris, A. J., 52, 54, 76, 99, 126
Hartley, J., 127
Heimlich, J. E., 148
Hidi, S., 176,
Highlighting, 76

Independence, fostering student, 23–26

Idol-Maestas, L., 205
Information:
    extracting, 4
    organizing, 5
INSERT, 75–76
Irvin, J. L., 207

Jacobsen, D. R., 127
James, J. H., 98
Johnston, P., 14
Jones, M. B., 178
Jones, R. S., 176, 178

Key words, 55–56
Kierwa, K., 126–127
Kinesthetic, 29
Knowledge:
    demonstrating, 5–6
    prior, 11
Koenke, K., 205
KWL, 178

Langer, J. A., 175
Learning:
    preferences, 29
    and remembering, 10–14
Lee, J. W., 52
Leverentz, F., 98
Listening:
    comprehension, 97–99
    promoting active, 99
    and reading comprehension, 98
    strategies to promote active, 99
    teaching, 98–99
Lundsteen, S. W., 98
Lyman, F. T., 15

Main ideas, 54–55
Maps:
    teaching, 149
    theoretical basis, 148–149
Marks, C., 176
Mason, J. M., 14
McAndrew, D. A., 76
McGee, L. M., 54
McKeown, M. G., 149, 207
McNeil, J. D., 176
McTighe, J., 15
Memory, 206–207
Metacognition, 11, 12-13, 73–74
    and studying, 12–13,

Mnemonics, 206–207
Modalities, 29–30
Moore, D. W., 148
Mountain, L. H., 148
Multiple-choice questions, 206

Nagy, W. E., 55, 207
Narrative text, 52–54
Nessel, D. D. 178
Newell, G. E., 175
Note-taking:
    research, 126–127
    teaching, 127–128
Noyce, R. M., 176

Ogle, D. M., 178
Olson, M. W., 53
Omanson, R. C., 149
Organizing:
    desks, 25
    at home, 28–29
    information, 5
    notebooks, 24
    students, 3–4, 25–26
    using charts, 128

Palincsar, A. S., 12, 176
Paris S. G., 11, 73, 74, 176
Pauk, W., 128
Pearson, P. D., 11, 14, 52, 98–99, 128, 149
Pittelman, S. D., 148
Previewing, 4, 52
Prewriting, 178
Pyramid desk organization, 25

Readance, J. E., 148
Reading:
    preparing students, 52–54
    promoting active, 72–74
Report writing, 177–179
    teaching, 178–179
Rickards, J. P., 127
Rickleman, R. J., 148
Ritter, S. 205
Robinson, F. P., 76
Roehler, L. R., 11, 77, 127

Schedules, following, 25–26
Schema theory, 11, 13–14
Schultz, C. B., 149

Scruggs, T. E., 205
Self-questioning, 74–75
Sinatra, R. C., 148
Singer, H., 74
Sipay, E. R., 52, 54, 76, 99, 126
Skimming, 57
Smith, P. L., 126, 127
SQ3R, 76–77
Stewart, O., 12, 74, 176
Sticht, T. G., 98
Strategic learning, 11–12,
Strategies defined 11
Strategies to promote active reading,
    74–77
  INSERT, 75–76
  self-questioning, 74–75
  SQ3R, 76–77
  underlining/highlighting, 76
Study skills:
  checklist, 6–9
  definition, 2
  extracting information, 4
  organizing information, 5
Summary writing, 175–177
  research, 176
  teaching, 176–177
Surveying, 4

Taylor, B. M., 53, 54, 176
Taylor, K. K., 54
Teacher, role of, 14–15
Tei, E., 12, 74, 176
Temple, C., 98, 99, 177, 178
Terry, C. A., 177
Test taking, 204–208

teaching test-taking skills, 205–206
  vocabulary, 207–208
Text:
  expository, 52–54
  kinds of, 52–54
  narrative, 52–54
  structure, 52
Think-Pair-Share, 15
Tompkins, G. E., 126, 127
Tonjes, M. J., 13, 127
TQLR, 99
True-false questions, 206
Turner, J. C., 11, 73, 176

Underlining/highlighting, 76
Understanding, demonstrating, 5–6
Unit approach, 26–28

Vacca, J. L., 13, 176
Vacca, R. T., 13, 176
van der Westhuizen, 73
Vaughn, J. L., 75
Vocabulary, 207–208

Wasik, B. A., 11, 73, 176
White, K. R., 205
Winograd, P. N., 54, 73, 74, 175, 176
Wittrock, M. C., 176
Writing:
  to learn, 174–175
  reports, 177–179
  summaries, 175–177

Zintz, M. V., 127